OXFORD
UNIVERSITY PRESS

CAMBRIDGE CHECKPOINT AND BEYOND

Complete English for Cambridge Secondary 1 Stage 7–9

Julian Pattison
Mark Pedroz

ASPIRE
SUCCEED
PROGRESS

WRITING AND GRAMMAR PRACTICE BOOK

Oxford excellence for Cambridge Secondary 1

OXFORD

Great Clarendon Street, Oxford, OX2 6DP, United Kingdom

Oxford University Press is a department of the University of Oxford.
It furthers the University's objective of excellence in research, scholarship, and education
by publishing worldwide. Oxford is a registered trade mark of Oxford University Press in the
UK and in certain other countries

British Library Cataloguing in Publication Data
Data available

978-0-19-837470-1

10 9

Paper used in the production of this book is a natural, recyclable product made from wood
grown in sustainable forests. The manufacturing process conforms to the environmental
regulations of the country of origin.

Printed and bound by CPI Group (UK) Ltd, Croydon, CR0 4YY

Acknowledgements

The publishers would like to thank the following for permissions to use their photographs:

p4: Marcus_Hofmann/Shutterstock; p8: Pedrosala/Shutterstock; p21: Wutthichai/Shutterstock;
p22: Kunal Mehta/Shutterstock; p25: Ouh_desire/Shutterstock; p32: Marynchenko Oleksandr/
Shutterstock; p36: Stephen Coburn/Shutterstock; p40: Mikhail Starodubov/Shutterstock; p45:
Sibrikov Valery/Shutterstock; p54: Morphart Creation/Shutterstock; p62: Breakermaximus/
Shutterstock; p64: Pedro Nogueira/Shutterstock; p66: PzAxe/Shutterstock; p70: Willyam
Bradberry/Shutterstock; p72: Jannoon028/Shutterstock; p76: Rawpixel.com/Shutterstock;
p82: Ajayptp/Shutterstock; p84: Rudall30/Shutterstock; p86: CoraMax/Shutterstock; p90:
Anna Jedynak/Shutterstock; p93: Alex Brylov/Shutterstock; p97: Click49/Shutterstock; p98:
ChakriPixmaker/Shutterstock; p100: Seita/Shutterstock; p102: Rudall30/Shutterstock; p106:
Anna Ponomarenko/Shutterstock; Artwork by Q2A Pvt. Ltd.

®IGCSE is the registered trademark of Cambridge International Examinations.

All sample questions and answers within this publication have been written by the authors.
In examination, the way marks are awarded may be different.

Contents

Introduction

How to use this book

Chapter 1 gives a brief reminder of grammar essentials with exercises to test your understanding. This is not intended to be a systematic explanation of how English grammar works. Nor does it provide a full set of exercises covering the complete range of grammatical confusions. Other books do these things. What it will give you is more explanation and practice of grammar issues as they arise in the **Complete English for Cambridge Secondary 1** Student Books (Stage 7, 8 and 9) and exercises that test your understanding.

You don't need to do the exercises in order, but you can concentrate on developing or revising particular skills on each page. If you work through the exercises in order, you will find that they move from essentials of grammar and constructing simple sentences, towards the choices you make over language and style, and ways to avoid common errors.

Chapter 2 will introduce you to – or remind you of – the rules for the whole range of punctuation in English. Once you have learned the rules, they soon become matters of habit and you will find that they help you to express yourself more clearly and flexibly in your own writing.

In **Chapters 3 to 5**, you will be given opportunities to practise the different genres of writing (fiction and non-fiction) featured in the Student Books. For each genre, you will be given a reminder of the basics to help you to make the right choices before you start to write. You are then encouraged to plan your writing and you are given advice on how to check and assess your work.

1. Planning your work

Good writing needs a plan or structure. For each genre covered, there is a planning grid for you to complete. To complete the planning grid:

- Think about how you will tackle the task you have chosen by considering each point in the planning grid.

- Write brief notes in the planning grid (or in your notebook) that you can build on when you start writing.

You can fill in the planning grid on your own, or with help from your friends or teacher, but remember that the final decisions need to be your own, because you want your writing to be personal and original.

2. Checking your work

It's always satisfying to finish a piece of writing, but it will be an even better piece if you check it by reading it through and making improvements. To help you to move on with your writing in this way, there is a checklist for you to complete before you submit your work:

- Using each point in the list, check your work.
- Make any improvements needed until you can tick every box in the checklist.

It is easy to make some improvements, especially when you are writing onscreen. You can also make handwritten corrections or additions. It is better than leaving the teacher to do this!

You can ask a friend to check your work, as long as you make the changes needed. You learn by finding out what your readers think about your writing.

3. Assessing your work

Assessment is not just your teacher giving you a mark or grade. The teacher's comments and corrections are there to help you to improve your work. Self-evaluation is the process of looking through your work when you receive it back from your teacher. It is the best way to improve your writing, so a checklist is provided for you to use for self-assessment. As you fill in the grid assessing your work in a particular genre, follow these steps:

- Consider what went well with your work: what are the strengths of your writing?
- Consider the weaknesses of your writing.
- Set yourself targets to help you improve next time you write in this genre.

By getting used to this way of checking your work, you will become aware of the skills you will need to develop, and you should be able to assess your own writing.

As your reach the end of this stage, you will naturally want to experiment more with your own use of English and prepare for the transition to IGCSE. **Chapter 6** gives you some pointers towards how you can move your skills on to the next level. It provides suggestions for how to develop your vocabulary and approach a text, even if you have never encountered anything like it before. The final section looks at common mistakes and how to avoid some of the most common errors in order to move forward.

Grammar

Simple sentences

Sentences are the building blocks of writing. You cannot construct a strong building unless you build it up from a well-constructed base. The basic building block is the single-clause sentence, which we often call a **simple sentence**. For example: Ibrahim opened the door.

This is a sentence, not a fragment, because it has a main verb. It also has a subject and an object. The subject 'governs' the verb; the object is the result of the verb. The verb is **transitive**.

Intransitive verbs can also make up simple sentences. For example:

Appears, seems, feels, looks like or *becomes* can also be main verbs, as can different parts of the verb *to be*.

Jamila cried out.

1. **Fill in the correct verb to complete the simple sentences below.**

   > **Remember**
   > A verb can be made out of more than one word.

   are performed   were borrowed   was   make   was born

   a William Shakespeare .... a famous English playwright, poet and actor.

   b He .... in the English town of Stratford-upon-Avon in 1564.

   c His plays .... all over the world.

   d Most of his stories .... from other sources.

   e His use of language and presentation of characters .... his writing unique.

2. **Simple sentences are effective ways to explain, to communicate information or to create tension in an exciting piece of writing. Turn the following paragraph into simple sentences by crossing out unnecessary conjunctions and adding full stops.**

   > Anjali and Paul approached the old farmhouse cautiously but they knew it was meant to be empty and they opened the cobweb-covered barn door and something dark flew out straight towards them but they recovered slowly from the shock then a man was standing in front of them and he was staring straight at them.

   ....

   ....

   ....

Simple sentences modified with adjectives and adverbs

Simple sentences are made more interesting by adding **adjectives** and **adverbs** (the parts of speech used for description). Understanding how adverbs are formed helps you with your spelling. You most often form an adverb by simply adding *–ly*.

If the adjective ends in *–y*, drop the *–y* and replace with *–i* before adding *–ly*. If the adjective ends *–le*, drop the final *–e* and add *–y*.

1. **Complete the following sentences by turning the adjective *quick*, *happy* or *simple* into an adverb.**

    a He was a *quick* bowler. He bowled ....

    b There was a *happy* ending. The story ended ....

    c She made a *simple* knot. She knotted the rope ....

2. **Turn these adjectives into adverbs then place the correct one into each sentence.**

accidental	full	terrible	steady	narrow

    a She walked .... along the dangerous ridge.

    b Tom .... dropped the slippery plate.

    c Adil thought the book ended ....

    d The team .... escaped defeat.

    e The class were told to answer the questions as .... as they could.

3. **Rewrite this paragraph, turning each adjective in brackets into an adverb. How do the adverbs make the apologies sound more sincere?**

    I am writing to apologise (full) for the mistake I made. I came into the classroom (noise) to fetch my bag. I did not realise the class inside were (silent) working on a test. I behaved (selfish) and (irresponsible).

    ....

    ....

    ....

    ....

    ....

Compound sentences

Even with adjectives and adverbs, simple sentences can be uninteresting because reading them is like reading a list. **Conjunctions** (or **connectives**) such as *or*, *and* or *but* can be used to join sentences together and make them more interesting.

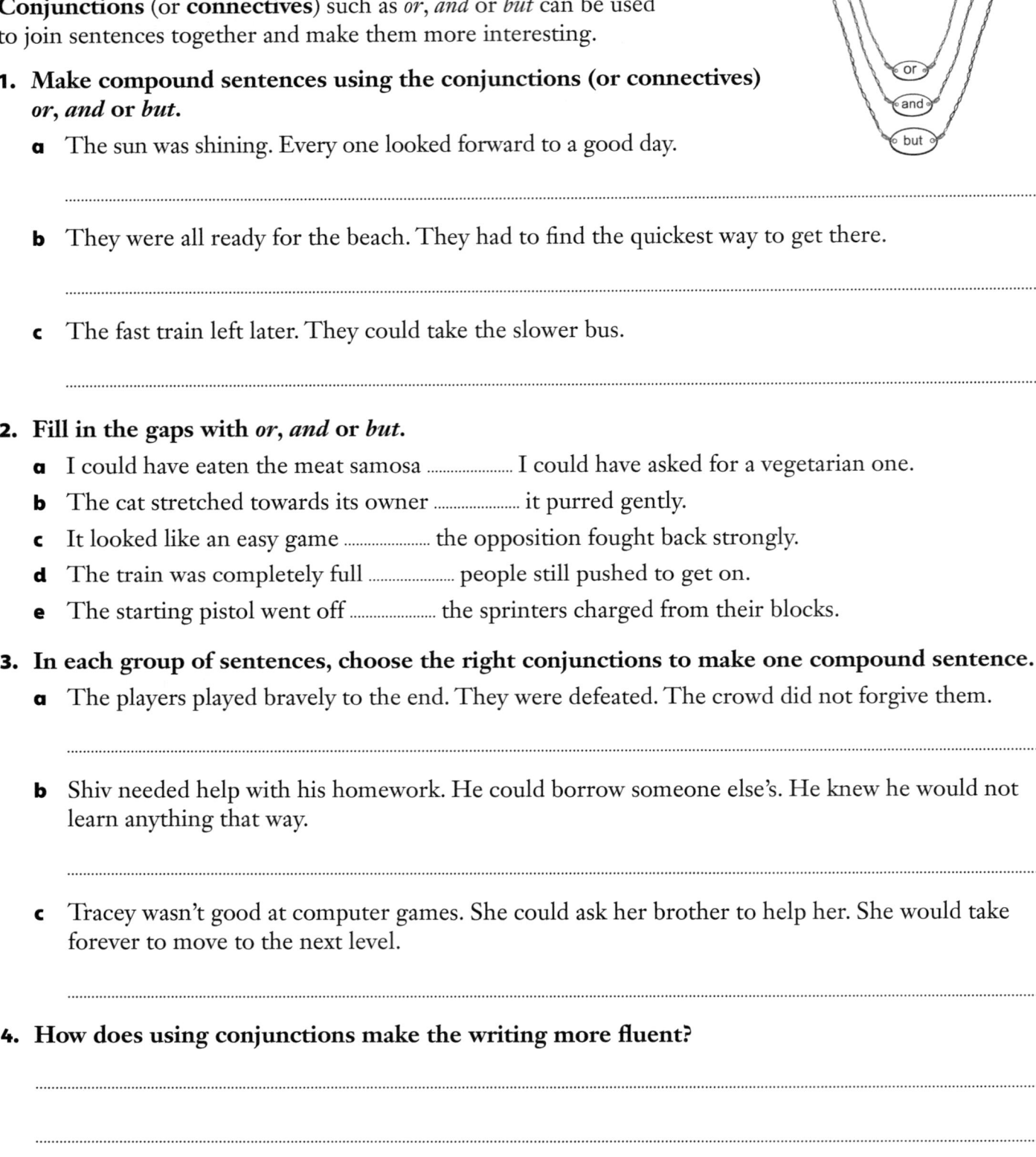

1. **Make compound sentences using the conjunctions (or connectives)** *or*, *and* **or** *but***.**

   a The sun was shining. Every one looked forward to a good day.

   ....

   b They were all ready for the beach. They had to find the quickest way to get there.

   ....

   c The fast train left later. They could take the slower bus.

   ....

2. **Fill in the gaps with** *or*, *and* **or** *but***.**

   a I could have eaten the meat samosa .... I could have asked for a vegetarian one.

   b The cat stretched towards its owner .... it purred gently.

   c It looked like an easy game .... the opposition fought back strongly.

   d The train was completely full .... people still pushed to get on.

   e The starting pistol went off .... the sprinters charged from their blocks.

3. **In each group of sentences, choose the right conjunctions to make one compound sentence.**

   a The players played bravely to the end. They were defeated. The crowd did not forgive them.

   ....

   b Shiv needed help with his homework. He could borrow someone else's. He knew he would not learn anything that way.

   ....

   c Tracey wasn't good at computer games. She could ask her brother to help her. She would take forever to move to the next level.

   ....

4. **How does using conjunctions make the writing more fluent?**

   ....

   ....

Using conjunctions and prepositions

Conjunctions are the words used to link sentences, such as: *although, before, because, if, in order to, since, though, unless, when.*
Prepositions come before a noun or pronoun to tell you about time, place or position, such as: *above, across, before, beside, between, during, from, in, off, on, since, through, until, without.*

Some words can be conjunctions or prepositions, depending on how you use them.

> **Remember**
> Varying your sentence lengths can be effective. Simple sentences create tension and **compound sentences** are good for more detailed explanation or description.

1. **Underline the conjunctions and prepositions in the sentences below. Decide if each is a 'preposition', a 'conjunction' or 'both'.**

   a He ran into the building. ....

   b The thieves bolted as he entered. ....

   c They had been there since one o'clock. ....

2. **Fill the gaps with a preposition or a conjunction. At the end of each sentence write whether you have used a preposition or a conjunction.**

   a The road passed .... the tunnel as the trains travelled over it. ....

   b .... it was already late, there was time to reach the post office before dark. ....

   c We said we would not turn up .... four o'clock. ....

   d Ugo sat .... the large man in the crowded train. ....

   e Khaled raced up the stairs .... get to his interview on time. ....

In many examples a preposition is followed by an **object pronoun** (*me, you, him, her, it, us* or *them*). In your writing you need to take care over the choice of prepositions.

3. **Circle the correct pronoun in the sentences below.**

   a We will keep this between *you and I/you and me*.

   b Their success went *before/beyond* expectations.

   c Cheese is made *of/from* milk.

   d The angry child snatched the toy car *off/from* his brother.

   e Shakespeare compared his beloved *with/to* a summer's day.

   f The group consisted *of/in* six old friends.

   g They walked *between/among* the tall grass.

   h There had been a big improvement *in/on* his attitude.

   i I agree *with/to* many of your ideas.

   j It was different *to/with* anything he had seen before.

Complex sentences (co-ordination and subordination)

Complex sentences link ideas using a range of conjunctions such as: *until, when, although, because, despite, whilst, whenever*. Some conjunctions go at the start of a sentence.

You can also use **relative pronouns** to link sentences: *that, which* or *who*.

1. **Circle the correct option in these sentences.**

   a She shuddered *because/despite* the creature seemed so malevolent.

   b *Although/When* Barbary apes have some humanoid characteristics, they are wild animals.

   c He shared some food with the frightened animal, *which/who* he pitied.

2. **Fill the gaps below with the correct conjunction or relative pronoun.**

   a .... many people think that Frankenstein is the name of a monster, this is not true.

   b Frankenstein was the name of the inventor .... made the monster.

   c In Mary Shelley's novel, Frankenstein has a happy childhood .... his mother's death makes him look for the secrets of life and death.

   d He neglects his family .... trying to create life from dead parts.

   e The creature is angry .... Frankenstein abandoned him in horror .... being his creator.

3. **Here is a set of notes for a speech. Rewrite them using compound sentences to make the speech fluent.**

> Genetically modified crops are sometimes called Frankenstein foods.
>
> Most scientists do not think genetically modified crops are intrinsically risky to human health.
>
> Genetically modified food has been around for 20 years.
>
> A GM tomato was first marketed in 1994.
>
> GM crops can be more disease resistant.
>
> They can produce higher yields.
>
> They could reduce the price of foodstuffs.
>
> They could produce cheap food for less wealthy parts of the world.
>
> There is a possibility of genetically modifying animal foodstuffs.
>
> No one is yet proposing this idea.

....

....

....

....

....

....

....

....

....

....

Subordinating conjunctions

In a complex sentence, the part that makes sense on its own is called the **main clause**. The **subordinate clause** depends on the main clause for its meaning.

The subordinate clause can come before or after the main clause. When the subordinating clause comes first, it needs to be separated from the main clause by a comma.

A **subordinating conjunction** always belongs at the beginning of a subordinate clause. Examples are: *after, although, as, because, before, even though, if, since, unless, until, when, whenever, whereas, wherever, while.*

> **Remember**
>
> A **relative pronoun** (which, that, whom, whose, when, where or who) separates the relative clause from the main clause. The **relative clause** always appears after the main clause.

1. Add the comma in the correct place in these sentences.

  a Although food is essential for our good health we need to be careful what we eat.

  b We need a balanced diet which consists of carbohydrate, proteins and unsaturated fats.

  c While the main food types are all essential they do need to be kept in the right balance as an excess of any one type can lead to health problems.

2. Complete the sentences below with a suitable conjunction.

a .... I was walking down the street, I saw a woman wearing a large hat.

b Karl passed the test .... he had prepared for it thoroughly.

c She did not want to go to Wales again .... she had plenty of wet weather clothing!

d .... she never liked the music, she had got used to hearing it every day.

e .... I did not want to turn back, I did not want to go on.

f .... you walked through the autumn woods, there were golden leaves brightening the gaps between the trees .... you looked.

g Ali found the task easy .... for Sunita it was much more difficult.

h .... I crossed the narrow strait to the island, I felt I had stepped into a different and happier world.

3. For each sentence in exercise 2, reverse the order of the clauses and add the correct punctuation. Make sure to keep the meaning the same.

a ....

b ....

c ....

d ....

e ....

f ....

....

g ....

h ....

....

Nouns and pronouns (first and third person)

When writing a narrative, you need to make a choice about who sees the action.

- Is someone looking from the outside, telling the story in the third person? (**objective** narrative)
- Is someone telling the story from his or her own point of view in the **first person**, as a character in the story? (**subjective** narrative)
- Does the writing combine the third person viewpoint with the limitations of a character's viewpoint? (**limited** narrative)

Whichever style you choose, you will need to make sure that the pronouns you choose match your choice of nouns.

1. Fill the gaps in the table with the correct pronoun.

	Subject	Object	Possession	
First person	I	me	my	Singular
Second person	you	you	your	Singular
Third person	she/he/it/one	her/ (a) ..../it	her/(b) ..../its	Singular
First person	(c)	us	our	Plural
Second person	you	you	your	Plural
Third person	they	(d)	their	Plural

2. Add the correct pronoun from the list in exercise 1.

a Lee and Su decided that .... would visit the city centre that morning.

b I wanted my parents to give .... a surprise for my birthday.

c You can find the tower when .... turn left and keep walking straight ahead.

d John could feel the tension rising, and knew .... would have to make his choice now.

e The police realised that .... best option was to wait until the gang surrendered.

3. Improve this report by adding pronouns instead of repeating the same names.

> Rick is making good progress in English. Rick's comprehension skills have improved. Rick can write good stories. However, spelling and punctuation need to improve and I have given Rick extra exercises to help Rick with this.
>
> Rick's class also visited the theatre where Rick's class enjoyed the play and meeting the actors. The class's reviews of the performance were lively and Rick's was the best of all.

....

....

....

....

Verbs and agreement

Just as nouns and pronouns need to agree, so must verbs and their subject. If you have a plural subject, you need a plural verb. If the subject is singular, the verb must be singular too. To decide whether the subject is singular or plural, look for the noun that governs the verb (the subject). A collective noun describing a group of things or people usually takes a singular verb.

The noun that governs a verb is not always the closest one to it.

1. **Circle the correct option from the paired words in these sentences.**

   a One of the students presented *her/their* findings to the rest of the class.

   b Members of the government made *their/its* decision.

   c Dominating the forest *were/was* the tall oak trees which had been there for hundreds of years.

2. **Fill the gaps by choosing the correct form of the verb. Use the context of the sentence to make sure you have the right tense.**

   a One of her favourite tracks (to be) .... the next one on the album.

   b They (to run) .... quickly down the street to catch their bus.

   c Dogs (to be) .... loyal animals and quite easy to train.

   d We (to want) .... to win, and to do it now!

   e The number of successful appeals against results (to have) .... increased.

3. **Rewrite the paragraph below correcting the errors. Pay particular attention to the verbs.**

   > Travelling to unusual countries give you a host of interesting stories as well as striking photographs. If you get talking, different people tells you the stories of their lives. Wandering off the tourist trail let you visit the shops and markets used by ordinary people. The sights and sounds is unusual and you will want to remember the smells and the taste of the food. Try anything once, is what I always says, and don't be afraid of the unfamiliar.
   >
   > For example, many believes different types of tea has health-given properties, and the experience are memorable, even if the taste can be unpalatable. Strong spices has the effect of turning a meal into an explosion of flavours, and I have experienced many meals which was cooked to perfection and impossible to imitate at home. Most cultures welcome tourists and brings you their tradition of hospitality to strangers, especially in the East.

   ....

   ....

   ....

   ....

   ....

   ....

   ....

   ....

Adjectives (comparatives and superlatives) and adjectival clauses

Adjectives can be adapted to form **comparatives** and **superlatives**. For example:

My attempt at the high jump was bad but Mayra's was worse and Jahan's was the worst.

Subordinate clauses can also be used to describe, using a subject and a verb. This is called an **adjectival clause**. These can be introduced by relative pronouns – *who, whom, whose, which, that* – or the pronoun can be understood, and left out to abbreviate the sentence. These are all ways to make your descriptive writing more varied and interesting. We call this **modification**.

> Be careful not to overuse adjectival clauses. Take care over punctuation too.

1. **Turn the adjective in brackets into a comparative or superlative.**

   a Ellen's presentation was better than Jo's, but Alice's was the (good) ....

   b Which of these two instruments makes the (loud) .... sound?

   c Many tried, but only the (brave) .... could stand more than a few minutes of the challenge.

2. **Fill the gap with the correct relative pronoun to complete the adjectival clause.**

   a I was confronted with a ravening beast .... was terrifying to look at.

   b The city, ... had towered over the plain for many centuries, was still many miles away.

   c Julian, ... had always been a good actor, made the most powerful impact on his audience.

   d Mari, to .... the lead part had been given, was very nervous.

   e The members of the orchestra, ... playing was normally so disciplined and harmonious, responded even more sensitively to her fine conducting.

3. **Read this descriptive piece of writing. In each sentence, underline the compound adjectives, circle adjectival clauses, and highlight comparatives and superlatives.**

> As the tsunami wave burst through the streets leading to the coast, people fled faster and more urgently. The destructive force of the water, advancing with terrifying speed, consumed everything in its path. Foamy-white water reared like horses threatening all in their wake. It was the scariest experience Arun had ever had. He clung to the concrete post, which gave him hope, and lashed a rope around both of them.

Adverbial phrases and adverbial clauses

Using adverbial phrases and adverbial clauses is another form of modification. Adverbial phrases and adverbial clauses are subordinate to the main verb, just as adjectival phrases are subordinate to the subject of a sentence.

We call these features **adverbial phrases** if they don't include a verb, or **adverbial clauses** if there is a subordinate verb. Like adjectival clauses, these can make compound sentences more descriptive and add detail to explanations.

They are linked to the main phrase using a conjunction.

1. **Match the purposes below to the correct conjunctions.**

a	time	**i**	so that
b	manner	**ii**	as soon as
c	place	**iii**	since
d	reason	**iv**	if
e	result	**v**	how
f	condition	**vi**	where
g	concession	**vii**	although

2. **Fill the gaps with a conjunction to form the adverbial clause.**

a .... I got to the school, I was already late.

b The young boy hurried through the tunnel .... burst confidently into the stadium.

c I needed to make a good impression .... I really wanted that job.

d Julia managed to abseil confidently down the slope .... her initial fears.

3. **Join these simple sentences using adverbial phrases. The result should be four sentences.**

> *Treasure Island* was written by Robert Louis Stevenson. It gives children the thrill of adult adventure. He chose Jack, a boy narrator. You feel Jack's terror and his growing confidence. He doesn't get much help from other adults. He finds a way to outwit the pirates. They fight among themselves. He thinks quickly and decisively. He can exploit this situation.

....

....

....

....

Managing tenses: regular and irregular verbs

Transforming sentences from present tense to past tense is often straightforward. We simply add *-ed* to the end of a verb. However, there are many **irregular verbs** that have a different form in the past tense, for example:

bend – bent	*fight – fought*	*lose – lost*
bring – brought	*get – got*	*make – made*
buy – bought	*hang – hung*	*spend – spent*
catch – caught	*have – had*	*stand – stood*
creep – crept	*hold – held*	*strike – struck*
deal – dealt	*keep – kept*	*teach – taught*
dig – dug	*lead – led*	*think – thought*
feed– fed	*learn – learnt*	*win – won.*
fall – fell	*leave – left*	

Some verbs take the same form in both the present tense and the past, for example: *bet; cast; hit; let; put; read; set; shut, split, spread, upset.*

1. Write the past tense for these verbs.

  a *meet* ....

  b *shine* ....

  c *tell* ....

2. Write the correct form of the past tense. (Not all the answers are above.)

  a I (dig) .... a large hole in the ground to hide the treasure.

  b In order to win, they (hold) .... onto their lead with strong defence.

  c We (stick) .... it out despite the cold, so we earned a warm drink when we got back.

  d We (bring) .... lots of presents so that our hosts would feel appreciated.

3. Rewrite this paragraph, changing the verbs from the present tense to the past tense.

> We keep the fishing rods in the shed and bring them out when we have a spare weekend. Many fish swim along this stretch of the river. We cast out our lines. The rods bend as the fish bite the bait. When we catch them, we slide them off the hook and place them back in the river. We leave when the sun goes down.

....

....

....

Active and passive voice

Some forms of writing need immediacy and urgency, so they use the **active voice**; others need a neutral or objective voice. When you need formality, or to create a sense of mystery, the **passive voice** can be useful. When using the passive voice, think about what is done rather than who did it.

Active voice:

Subject	Verb	Object
Both children	saw	a bright light in the sky

Passive voice:

Object	Verb	Subject
A bright light in the sky	was seen	by both children

In the example above, changing from the active to the passive puts the emphasis on the mysterious object (a bright light in the sky) and the fact that there were two witnesses (both children). Is the object or the subject more important?

1. **Decide if each sentence below is active or passive, by writing 'A' or 'P' next to each one.**

   a The new film was released in many cinemas last night. ....

   b The car crashed into the barrier. ....

   c The class were congratulated on another fine set of essays. ....

2. **Fill in the correct form of the verb, whether active or passive.**

   a The students (give) .... the instruction to start their exam.

   b Mo (play) .... centre forward in the team for many years.

   c We walked slowly across the field where large cows (graze) ....

   d The window (broken) .... by one of you.

   e Meera (give) .... the signal that she was ready to start the experiment.

3. **Convert these sentences from the active to the passive voice.**

a Carl received news of his university place this morning.

....

b His father mowed the lawn every Sunday.

....

c The burglars had forced the door open.

....

d The manager did not give a satisfactory reason for the team's performance.

....

....

e The laboratory technician observed a white precipitate as the silver nitrate was added.

....

....

Adverbial and adjectival phrases

Clauses require verbs but phrases do not. Adverbial phrases do the same job as adverbs – they describe verbs – but they add some extra detail. Similarly, **adjectival phrases** describe nouns. Both give sentences modification. Think about what modification adds to your writing and consider which kinds of writing it is suitable for, and which it is not.

1. **Decide if the phrase in the sentence is 'Adverbial' or 'Adjectival'.**

a Rather surprisingly, we went ahead with the plan. ....

b They found the answers extremely quickly. ....

c The teacher thought their excuses were simply unconvincing. ....

2. **Add adverbial or adjectival phrases to make your description more interesting.**

    a He launched himself .... into the midst of the combat.

    b That answer is .... ridiculous!

    c She said he was behaving .... by putting them in danger.

    d They moved .... from one routine to the next.

    e Taking us by surprise, our opponents .... changed their positions.

3. **Add interest to this account of a school trip by adding adverbial and adjectival phrases. They can add more of your emotions to your report. Fill the gaps with more than one word.**

> Despite heavy rain and growing darkness, the minibus was driven (a) ....
>
> towards our destination. Stepping out, we were struck by the (b) ....
>
> quiet of our distant destination. The farmhouse loomed (c) .... over
>
> us. However, once we were inside we (d) .... organised our sleeping
>
> arrangements while the teachers lit a (e) .... fire.
>
> We (f) .... turned the house into our home for the next four days, and
>
> gathered round the fire to tell each other different kinds of (g) ....
>
> stories. We felt (h) .... and appreciated this would be the ideal
>
> environment to develop our creative writing and work (i) .... together. If
>
> you get the chance, take this (j) .... opportunity to get away from school
>
> and learn to write in a very different environment from the classroom!

Conditionals and modals

Conditionals and **modals** allow you to explore a world of possibilities. They address things that have not happened yet, but could or should happen in the future. There are different levels of possibility.

1. **For each option given below, choose the correct one and underline it.**

    a Something is going to happen if the condition is met:

        If they turn up, they *will/might/should* find us waiting to surprise them.

    b Something will probably happen if the condition is met:

        If they turn up, they *will/might/should* find us waiting to surprise them.

    c Something might possibly happen if the condition is met:

        If they turn up, they *will/might/should* find us waiting to surprise them.

In exercise 1, each sentence expresses a different likelihood that the meeting will happen. If you put the conditional in the past tense, it becomes a possibility that never happened. For example:

If they had turned up, we could have surprised them.

The most common modal auxiliary verbs in order of likelihood are: *will, would, shall, should, need, ought (to), can, could, may, might.* For past repeated actions we say 'used to'.

> The past tense is *could have* or *should have* or *could've* or *should've* **never** *could of* or *should of.*

2. **Fill the gap with the correct auxiliary verb in each sentence.**

a .... you remember how we sorted out this problem last time?

b There .... be problems up the line which made the train late.

c It's a waste of time going back over what .... have been.

d Candidates .... put their name in the box provided.

e Something really .... to be done about it!

3. **In this report, the wrong auxiliaries have been used. Can you correct them?**

> Anil (a) **should** be a good student of English but has done little work to show this. He (b) **shall** improve his writing by paying more attention to punctuation and grammar. I (c) **may** give him some extra exercises for practice over the vacation. These (d) **might** be completed before the next term. More systematic reading (e) **need** develop his lively imagination in a more disciplined way, and (f) **shall** improve his creative writing. If he (g) **ought to** work harder on basic skills, and if he develops a more sophisticated vocabulary, he (h) **might** be capable of higher grades as he (i) **may** give intelligent responses in class discussion. It (j) **may** give us all pleasure to see him succeed.

a ....

b ....

c ....

d ....

e ....

f ....

g ....

h ....

i ....

j ....

Prefixes and suffixes

Using **prefixes** and **suffixes** is a good way of building more complex nouns. Once you recognise frequent prefixes and suffixes, it becomes easier to spell longer words correctly. Prefixes and suffixes are added to the stem of a word.

1. Complete the gaps below with a prefix or suffix to make a correct word.

Prefix	Stem	Suffix
dis	appear	*–ance*
un	happi (*y* is modified)	*–ly*
in	sincer (*e* is removed)	*–ity*
in	complete	
(a)	necessary	
dis	agree	(c) ....
(b)	eligible	

Negative prefixes, such as the ones in exercise 1, are especially common ways of modifying the meaning of nouns. Other negative prefixes are *im–*, *ir–*, *il–* and *mis–*. The suffixes *–ed* and *–ing* modify verbs.

2. Add the correct negative prefix to each stem.

a .... literate   **c** .... mortal   **e** .... natural

b .... reparable   **d** .... spelt

There are many more prefixes, such as: *sub–, under–, over–, re–, pre–, super–, fore–, ex–, extra–, with–*.

There are also many suffixes other than *–ed* and *–ing*, such as: *–ion, –ation, –ful, –ment, –ance, –ence, –ive, –less, –ly, –ally, –ous, –eous, –able*.

> Recognising the prefix in a word can help you to remember that you must double the consonants.

3. Use the correct prefixes and suffixes to fill the gaps in the sentences.

a Women have been outrag .... ly .... represented at executive level.

b He had .... conscious intuit .... that this situation would be danger ....

c She travelled as a .... numerary passenger on the impress .... tanker.

d The disappear .... of the Marie Celeste's crew was .... ordinary.

e The disgrace .... coward .... shown by the guards made them .... trusted.

Synonyms and antonyms

Using **synonyms** and **antonyms** is one way of varying your vocabulary by finding more unusual words. A dictionary of synonyms and antonyms, such as a thesaurus, will develop your vocabulary. However, be careful to ensure that the word you choose as a synonym or antonym means what you think it means.

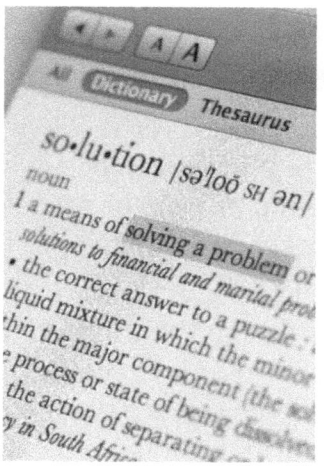

1. **Write 'S' or 'A' alongside these pairs of words to indicate whether they are synonyms or antonyms.**

   a bulletin   report   ....
   b prudent   reckless   ....
   c shop   emporium   ....

2. **Underline the word that means the same or nearly the same as the word in bold.**

   a **courageous**   fortunate   supine   bold   wild

   b **mislead**   deceive   deceitful   deceptive   disingenuous

   c **melody**   harmony   music   discord   tune

   d **forage**   forward   promote   hit   hunt

   e **consolation**   prize   condolence   pity   conference

3. **Underline the word or words which mean the opposite, or nearly the opposite, of the word in bold.**

   a **content**   unhappy   delighted   tragic   uncontent

   b **disparage**   talk down   talk up   discount   page

   c **intuitive**   instinctive   tuition   tutor   taught

   d **impassive**   fortunate   exciting   active   emotional

   e **exceptional**   frequent   ordinary   friendly   outstanding

   f **inconsolable**   happy   competent   fashionable   indignant

   g **ecstatic**   high   static   miserable   understandable

   h **prominent**   hollow   empty   important   unobtrusive

   i **vain**   lazy   kind   humble   careless

   j **excessive**   too strong   too little   too successful too much

Prepositions and prepositional phrases

Phrases don't need verbs. They are parts of sentences, but lack a verb. Phrases can be adverbial phrases, adjectival phrases, noun phrases or prepositional phrases, depending on whether they do the work of adverbs, adjectives, nouns or prepositions.

First, here's a quick reminder of the function of a **preposition**: the prefix *pre–* reminds you that the word comes *before* a noun or pronoun. The stem *position* reminds you that the word is concerned with position, place or time.

Prepositions make links and relations between different parts of a sentence. They help you to extend sentences.

1. **Here are some descriptive, complex and compound sentences based on journeys. Fill the gap with a suitable preposition.**

   a They carefully made their way .... the quick-flowing river.

   b Hu climbed .... the top of the rock, so that he could see how far he had travelled.

   c It had been a long and tiring ascent .... lunch, and they still had had further to go before reaching their goal.

A **prepositional phrase** uses part of a sentence as a preposition in order to tell you more about a noun. There is a preposition in front of a noun phrase. If a prepositional phrase appears at the beginning of a sentence, it is always followed by a comma. Use prepositional phrases in writing to extend your use of descriptions.

2. **Underline the prepositional phrase in these sentences.**

   a You will find the castle behind that hill and across the valley.

   b On the other side of the narrow bridge over the highway, you will find the old town.

   c Under such circumstances, their slow progress was not surprising.

   d Sheng trudged through the rain-soaked marshes, well-protected by waterproof boots.

   e The railway wound its way slowly over the steep incline of the mountainous region.

3. **Add a suitable preposition to introduce the prepositional phrase.**

   a .... ominously gathering rainclouds, they prepared a warm breakfast before setting off.

   b We need to get back .... the gates are locked or we won't be able to get out.

   c Their way lay .... broad and rolling plains which would be a comfortable ride.

   d .... the breaking waves lay a long and inviting beach, ideal to spend a rest day.

Phrasing in sentences (in parenthesis)

Look at this simple sentence: Jai crossed the stream.

Now answer these questions, which are based on expanded versions of the sentence.

1. **Underline the following in the sentence below.**

   a Underline the prepositional phrase.   **b** Underline the adverb.

   In the cool shade of the woodland, Jai tentatively crossed the gurgling stream.

   c Now underline the adjectival phrase that has been added:

   In the cool shade of the woodland, Jai, an instinctively cautious boy, tentatively crossed the gurgling stream.

We could also call this adjectival phrase a **parenthetical phrase**. It is closely linked to the main clause, but the sentence would make sense without it. You could put brackets around the phrase – or dashes for emphasis – while commas draw less attention to it. This is an example of how punctuation can keep long sentences under control.

Word order helps you with phrasing. Just as you keep adjectives close to the noun they describe, keep adverbs near the verbs or adjectives they describe. Word order can also affect a sentence's meaning.

2. **Punctuate and order these sentences correctly.**

   a Quickly my business-like but confident that he knew what he was looking for father through the various channels his way zapped.

   ....

   ....

   b Animatedly waving their arms in the air marching across old battlefields explained the history behind them dully-dressed experts.

   ....

   ....

   c Seizing the controller asked my mother briskly walking across the living room "Can't we watch something else".

   ....

   ....

d Vacuous celebrities the screen suddenly was filled with exchanging movie stars gossip about.

....

....

e Going upstairs I said I was where waiting for me my laptop was from my friends full of messages and pictures glowing.

....

....

3. **Change the word order of the extract below so that it reads correctly. Your answer should have three clauses.**

> The victorious powers ensured peace treaties were signed, despite their humiliating terms of surrender, by forcing defeated nations to the conference.

....

....

4. **How does changing the order of words in exercise 3 change the meaning?**

....

....

Sentence variation

You have learnt ways of constructing longer sentences, but it is also important to remember to end them. Short, simple sentences have a powerful effect. They highlight what is most important. Students often make the mistake of not stopping a sentence, and using commas instead of full stops. This is sometimes called the 'comma splice'.

> **Remember**
>
> If there are two main verbs in a sentence you need either a full stop or a connective that turns the second part into an adjectival clause.

1. **Correct sentence separation is essential. For each sentence below, place a tick if the punctuation is correct, or a cross if it is wrong.**

   a They passed through the portal, it was a gateway to an entirely different world. ....

   b They passed through the portal. It was a gateway to an entirely different world. ....

   c They passed through the portal, as it was a gateway to an entirely different world. ....

2. **Correct the following incorrect sentences by adding a full stop in the right place. Some sentences will need a comma too.**

   a I always find writing stories difficult I tend to leave the task to the last minute.

   ....

   b Ben preferred to have a light on when he went to bed he was afraid of the dark.

   ....

   c He woke up to find his body distending and his arms and legs shrunken he had become a giant beetle.

   ....

   d As the Lilliputians thought about the huge size of the giant they realized how they could make him useful he could help them win their war against the Blefuscans their old enemies.

   ....

   e Digging further beneath the surface they discovered the traces of a much older city there were ancient bricks and curious fragments of pottery and metal.

   ....

3. **Which form of punctuation could also divide these main clauses while still showing that they are linked?**

   ....

   ....

Formal and informal register

As you get closer to IGCSE, you will find you are asked to write in a greater variety of styles. You will spend more time writing arguments, supported by evidence, as well as stories (narratives) and descriptions. Your language will need to be appropriate for your audience. You will need to decide whether the **register** (both vocabulary and grammatical style) should be formal or informal.

1. **Look at the list below. Rank these pieces of writing in order of formality, where 1 is the most formal.**

   a A speech to your classmates ....

   b A letter to a friend ....

   c A report to a committee of teachers and other adults. ....

2. **Decide if the register used in each example below is formal (F) or informal (I).**

   a I regret to inform you that this account is now overdrawn and I must request that this receive your serious attention. ....

   b It was an amazing day! Thanks so much and let's do it again. ....

   c "I dinna ken," said the Scotsman, and if he didn't know the way, we certainly didn't. ....

   d Our perambulation concluded with a detailed inspection of the works. ....

   e You'll want to be on the winning side of this argument, won't you? ....

3. **Decide if these elements of grammar and vocabulary are most likely to appear in a formal (F) or informal (I) piece of writing.**

   a abbreviation ....   **f** dialogue ....

   b slang or dialect ....   **g** complex sentences ....

   c synonyms with many syllables ....   **h** parenthetical phrases ....

   d the passive voice ....   **i** modal verbs ....

   e exclamations and rhetorical questions ....   **j** indirect or reported speech ....

Looking back, you will see that many of the grammar skills you have been practising are especially important for formal writing. However, informal writing also requires correct punctuation and grammatical structure, even though the vocabulary and sentence structures will probably be less complex.

Abbreviation

You will want to use abbreviations in dialogue and less formal writing so that your language fits your audience and purpose. It's important to use abbreviation correctly. We usually signal abbreviation through full stops: *e.g., i.e., M.A., Prof.*. Nevertheless, some common abbreviations do not need full stops: *Mr, Mrs, Dr*, for example.

We signal missing letters in a word by using an apostrophe, but the apostrophe is also used to indicate possession and the plurals of letters and numbers. For further guidance, turn to Chapter 2 on punctuation, but knowledge of grammar can help to avoid common errors.

1. Correct the following sentences.

 a In two years' time its going to be a leap year.

 ....

 b It should of been Lohit's turn next.

 ....

 c I didnt think you'd call me.

 ....

Words that sound similar can indicate abbreviation or possession.
Abbreviation takes precedence (it comes first in the alphabet).

2. **Think about where a verb has been left out and underline the correct option to start these sentences.**

 a *Who's/Whose* going to take the chance?
 b *Who's/Whose* coat is this?
 c *Theirs/There's* plenty to do this evening.
 d *They're/Their/There* place is on the right-hand table.
 e *Your/You're* going to be my teacher next term.

Another common confusion arises over modal verbs. They can be abbreviated: *could have – could've, would have – would've, should have – should've*. Again, a verb has been left out, and this must not be confused with possession (*could of, should of, would of* are incorrect).

3. **Make sure the apostrophes correctly signal abbreviation in the following sentences. There are some possessive apostrophes and deliberate mistakes too, in order to test your skills further. Underline the mistakes, then write the corrected words beside each sentence.**

 a Theyve gone to see the leopards and tigers in the big cats enclosure. ....
 b Dont say youve got into trouble again. Your such an embarrassment! ....
 c Lets see what their going to say about are arguments now. ....
 d You could of told me you werent going to show up. ....
 e Im not going to say any more because its not my responsibility. ....

Possessives and relatives

We have seen that you can avoid mistakes by not confusing abbreviation with pronouns. This is a good moment to revise **possessive pronouns**. This table shows what you need to remember.

	Singular	Plural
First person	mine	ours
Second person	yours	yours
Third person	his/hers/its	theirs

1. **In the following sentences, replace the text in brackets with a pronoun to avoid unnecessary repetition.**

   a That's Darsh's exercise book. (Indira's) exercise book is on the teacher's desk. ....

   b It's time for us to have our turn. You've had (your turn). ....

   c Our train still hasn't arrived. (Their train) is already waiting at its platform. ....

Other forms of pronoun are **relative pronouns** and **demonstrative pronouns**. Like possessive pronouns, these are used a lot in informal writing but they mustn't be muddled with abbreviations.

Relative pronouns are: *who, whom, whose, that, which*.

Demonstrative pronouns are: *that, this, those, these*.

2. **Choose the correct relative or demonstrative pronoun to complete these sentences.**

   a Tife asked to .... the tickets belonged.

   b The nurses, ... bravery had been obvious in dealing with the epidemic, were given awards.

   c .... are sad-looking flowers!

   d He made a discovery .... has made a difference by saving many lives.

   e .... is the best time we've had for ages!

Pronouns can be used in questioning (*who, whose, which* and *to/for whom*) and reflexive statements (*myself, yourself, his, her, itself* and *ourselves, yourselves, themselves*).

3. **Underline the pronouns in this sentence, and then explain the use of each.**

   Which of you will prove yourselves women by standing up for those who aren't allowed to speak out?

   ....

   ....

   ....

   ....

Pronouns and antecedents

We have seen how pronouns, like abbreviations, are powerful ways of linking your argumentative writing more directly to speech, which can work well in informal contexts. However, you always need to make sure that pronouns are linked closely to their **antecedents**. Keep the grammar of the sentence securely in mind.

1. Add the correct pronoun to each gap. The first one is done for you.

Antecedent		Pronoun
Nelson Mandela	pardoned those who imprisoned him,	which showed his commitment to peace and reconciliation.
Thousands of people	have benefited from the discovery of antibiotics	that have cured (a) .... of infection.
As opponents to change	who want to protect your own income and security,	(b) .... are not going to convince me we shouldn't do something to help refugees.
I am telling you	many others feel as passionate about our planet as I do,	and that should make you want to join (c) .... campaign for all our futures.

2. Sometimes the antecedent to a pronoun is another pronoun. Cross out the incorrect pronoun in these sentences and write the correct one alongside.

   a Bo told us to say that the work had been done by I and you. ....

   b Whenever I tried to tell them off, them wouldn't listen to me. ....

   c We wanted to play outside but it rained all day so their games had to be indoor ones. ....

   d Between you and me, them don't have any chance of winning it. ....

   e I'm not going to tell you what to do, that's for us to decide. ....

3. Make sure you don't confuse the reader by using too many pronouns. There are six errors in the following paragraph. Can you find them?

> Juan and Angela were playing outside. Their father Adolfo was indoors reading a book. He put it down and asked him if he would like some sandwiches. He said that was just what he needed, so he made some sandwiches. When he came back, he and Angela were using badminton rackets. When they finished, they packed them up and he gave them them.

....

....

....

....

Expanding vocabulary: compound nouns and homonyms

Words can be combined to form compound nouns. **Compound nouns** can be made up of two nouns, or combinations of verb and noun, adjective and noun, preposition and noun, and verb and preposition.

Some need a hyphen: *We are going to visit our mother-in-law.*

Some do not: *It's time I had a haircut.*

In others the words are kept separate: *I recorded it on a compact disc.*

There's no rule: look out for common practice when you are reading, and learn!

Pronunciation (or stress) needs to be different to distinguish these words from adjectives and nouns. Compound adjectives always need a hyphen: *swimming-pool attendant, a nineteenth-century poem.*

1. **Using the clues given, add the compound nouns needed in these sentences.**

    a We need to collect the .... (term that describes a way of cleaning delicate fabrics).

    b It's time I stopped having to share a .... (room to sleep in).

    c We should make sure the hotel has a .... (place to swim).

Another problem is words that sound the same (**homonyms**) or nearly the same, but have different meanings. You must think about the meaning when spelling the word, not just the sound. Learn from your reading!

2. **Underline the correct word in each sentence.**

    a The audience were strongly *effected/affected* by the performance.

    b It was the best *compliment/complement* she had ever been paid.

    c The poem made complex *allusions/illusions* to past events.

    d An *elicit/illicit* trade in ivory causes the death of many elephants.

3. **Again, underline the correct word in each sentence.**

    a He gave her clear and *implicit/explicit* instructions.

    b Many think that bullfighting is an *inhuman/inhumane* sport.

    c The judge was entirely *disinterested/uninterested* in her task.

    d There are a number of points of *principal/principle* here.

Sometimes, it's best to use a dictionary to avoid confusing words that seem similar.

Paragraphing: connectives and topic sentences

In longer pieces of argued writing, you need to pay attention to paragraphing. You should change **paragraph** when you change subject. If a paragraph is very long, split it by introducing a new point. If it is too short, try to develop your point with a piece of evidence, an anecdote or an example. Indent or leave a line to signal the change of paragraph.

Connectives help you to shape your paragraphs.

> **Remember**
>
> It is usually better to use connectives in the **topic sentence**. There should be a comma nearby, too!

1. **Write these three words in the correct column in the table.**

   a *nevertheless* **b** *therefore* **c** *additionally*

Develop	Contrast	Conclude
moreover, consequently, equally	however, yet, despite this	finally, lastly, as a result

2. **Underline the correct connective in each topic sentence.**

   a The death penalty satisfies our feelings of natural justice, *nevertheless/moreover* it is the strongest possible deterrent.

   b We have seen the catastrophic failure of banks and markets to withstand crisis, *consequently/ subsequently* there is a strong case for the state to take more control of the economy.

   c School uniforms prevent distracting fashion competitions, *equally/however* they also avoid unpleasant distinctions between richer and poorer families.

   d *Finally/by contrast*, even my opponents must agree that homework, in whatever form, is a support to learning.

3. **Topic sentences establish your subject, the genre you have chosen and the content of what follows. Decide if the following are topic sentences, by writing 'Yes' or 'No' next to each one.**

   a His characters were popular because of their larger-than-life qualities. ....

   b Dickens was an enormously successful writer in his lifetime. ....

   c It was a dark, gloomy night and wind whistled down the chimney. ....

   d Out of the darkness glimmered a pale light, and they heard a sound. ....

   e We can, alternatively, consider some of the benefits of wind turbines. ....

More on linking sentences: phrasal connectives

Let's explore some more ways in which we link and connect ideas, in order to sequence sentences and paragraphs. Phrasal connectives make links through phrases rather than words. These also have different functions.

1. **Write the following words in the correct box.**

    a *even though*   **b** *all things considered*   **c** *exclusive of*

Time / sequence	by the time that	**Repetition**	above all	**Exception**	With the exception of
	at last		in other words		other than
	in the past/ future		as a matter of fact		except for the fact that
	last but not least		as was said earlier		outside of
Reason/ purpose	in order that/to	**Concession**	granted that	**Compare/ contrast**	in the same way
	for this purpose/reason		it may be true that		in a similar way
	to this end		and yet		despite the fact that
	that being the case		of course		for all that

2. **Underline the correct phrasal connective in each sentence below.**

    a *Despite/Except for* the fact that many think hunting cruel, it is an important part of rural life.

    b *Above all/To this end*, I ask you to support the proposition.

    c *Granted that/to this end* there are good arguments on either side.

    d We all agree *with the exception of/in the same way* as a small minority.

    e *And yet/That being the case*, let's look at a further reason for action.

3. **You are preparing a debating speech to your class, presenting your own reasons and evidence for supporting or opposing a proposition (a 'motion'). Choose your motion, and then (in your notebook) organise your ideas into short paragraphs, using phrasal connectives. If you can, work with a partner who can present the counter argument, using the same techniques.**

Ordering sentences for effect

First, we need to avoid ambiguity and confusion. For example:

The man was talking to a companion. He was about thirty.

This could be rewritten as:

The man, who was about thirty, was talking to a companion.

Or it could be written as:

The man was talking to a companion, who was about thirty.

1. What is the most likely way to sort out these confusing sentences? Write your version beneath each one.

   a The football players were talking to the fans. They were overawed.

   ....

   b The old man sat next to the boy. He was smoking a pipe.

   ....

   c The police questioned the youths about the incidents the previous evening. They were very embarrassed.

   ....

Longer sentences, punctuation and relative clauses help to avoid ambiguity. Word order can also be used for emphasis, or to make your meaning more clear and elegant.

2. Reorganise these sentences for maximum impact. Write your version beneath each one.

   a Tigers can be seen in their natural habit in this country.

   ....

   b The best time to see animals gathering around the waterhole is sunrise.

   ....

   c All around them was wilderness as they waited for rescue.

   ....

3. **Analyse each of the ten different kinds of sentence in this extract and explain their effect.**

> Safari is unique. We all enjoy the opportunity to see wild and dangerous animals close up. Wouldn't you appreciate this more, if they were on their native soil, rather than a zoo? Lions, leopards and cheetahs are just some of the animals you can find in Nairobi safari park, even though it is only just outside the busy city. There are rhinoceros and elephants too. Nearby you will find an elephant sanctuary, where orphaned elephants are cared for. Other abandoned and orphaned animals, who can therefore never return to the wild, are looked after in a part of the park dedicated to them. They live in their natural habit, but can be supervised – and you can visit them easily. More adventurous and exciting is the chance to see animals truly wild. For this, however, you will need to be up early and it is best to have a guide who will find the locations which will be safe, yet give you a good chance to spot the big beasts.

....

....

....

....

....

....

....

....

....

....

....

....

....

....

Rhetorical strategies

Rhetorical strategies that influence word order and the organisation of ideas and sentences include **alliteration**, **inversion**, **parallelism** and **tricolon**.

1. **Each of the sentences below includes one of the rhetorical strategies mentioned. Underline it and write 'alliteration', 'inversion', 'parallelism' or 'tricolon' next to the sentence.**

   a   Sometimes it was easy, sometimes it was tough. ....

   b   We will fight on with our hands, with our minds and with our hearts. ....

   c   Never was so much owed to so many people working together. ....

   d   Keep playing with speed, superiority and spirit! ....

Notice how each of the sentences in exercise 1 sounds like a conclusion: that is the place where you most need rhetorical strategies.

2. **Identify the rhetorical strategies used in the following famous advertising slogans. Write the correct term alongside each example.**

   a   Power, beauty and soul. (Aston Martin) ....

   b   Save Money. Live Better. (Walmart) ....

   c   Impossible is Nothing. (Adidas) ....

   d   Solutions for a smart planet. (IBM) ....

   e   Keeps going and going and going. (Energizer) ....

It is also important, finally, to vary your sentences and style. Expand your vocabulary by reading a variety of fiction and non-fiction texts. Never, lose sight of the importance of writing concisely, with clarity. Attention to grammar helps you to avoid error, yet also makes your writing more interesting.

Words to avoid are: *nice, well, boring, OK, good, bad, positive, negative.* These are so overused that they have become meaningless.

Also avoid the common error of **pleonasm**, which is unnecessary repetition and padding.

3. **Cross through the unnecessary words in this extract, to make it more clear and interesting.**

> We were totally and utterly unanimous in agreeing that this was outrageous. We had seen it with our own eyes and knew her self-defence of herself was over-exaggerated and her excuse was not sufficient enough to justify what she did.

2 Punctuation

Why punctuate?

Here are two versions of an extract. Try reading each one aloud. Is it easier to read the first version or the second?

1. the main reason for punctuation is to be friendly to your reader it helps to eliminate possible misunderstandings it also helps the reader understand the flow of your sentence for example you are saying two different things in the sentences lets eat grandma and lets eat grandma

2. The main reason for punctuation is to be friendly to your reader. It helps to eliminate possible misunderstandings, and it helps the reader understand the flow of your sentence. You are saying two different things in the following sentences:

   'Let's eat, grandma'; 'Let's eat grandma'.

Remember

Use capital letters:

- to begin sentences
- for proper nouns (nouns that name a specific place, person or item)
- for important words in titles (Puss in Boots)
- for special days in the year (Ramadan, Independence Day)
- for days and months (Friday 3 December)
- for yourself: I don't agree.

---

1. **Write out these sentences with corrections so that they make sense.**

   a i've never heard of pink Elephants. Loose on the road. Before?

   ....

   b I want to buy apples and pears! When I go shopping in the market.

   ....

   c noor flew to new york. And paris. Last year.

   ....

   d Crying won't. Help you it's – broken.

   ....

   e 'pirates Of The Caribbean' Is my favourite film?

   ....

Full stops and sentences

Full stops	• show the end of a sentence	She had travelled widely in Asia before settling in Singapore.
	• show abbreviation (but this is slightly old-fashioned)	Mr. Khan has a B.A. from the university. He works for the U.N.

> To introduce something new, start a new sentence.

The best way to check where full stops are needed is to read aloud. When something new is being introduced, a new sentence should start.

It was a dark and stormy night. The old man decided that he would go to bed early. The wind was starting to blow strongly outside. He felt very alone.

Four separate points are made here. Each is a separate sentence because there is a verb with tense (telling you when it happened) and indication of number (telling you how many people or things were involved).

1. **Rewrite these sentences, adding full stops and capital letters where they are needed.**

   a we went to argentina for our holiday I wanted to sample the food my mother and sister wanted to learn the tango my brother was keen to see the football

   ....

   ....

   b my father works in bangalore he is 40 years old my mother is 38 they both have full-time jobs

   ....

   ....

   c the school magazine has been printed it is available from the office it can be sent out by post if requested many of the students have contributed articles or artwork

   ....

   ....

   d i like to watch television in the evening my favourite programmes are soap operas i never watch the news i never watch during the day i have too much to do

   ....

   ....

More practice with full stops

1. **Read this extract and then insert full stops where they are needed.**

> Victoria Falls was first seen by Europeans in 1855 it is 1708 metres wide and 108 metres high it is the largest sheet of falling water in the world it is on the Zambezi river Victoria Falls is also called by its original name Mosi-oa-Tunya the falls is at the border between Zambia and Zimbabwe it is now a popular tourist destination about a million tourists visit each year the falls can easily reached by bus and train the area round the falls is popular for adventure sports

2. **Here is the same content, written differently. Rewrite the extract, adding capital letters and full stops where they are needed. This time, you might also need some commas if the sentences pause without quite seeming complete.**

> Victoria Falls on the Zambezi river is 1706 metres wide and 108 metres high and is the largest sheet of falling water in the world on the border between Zimbabwe and Zambia Victoria Falls is also known by its original name Mosi-oa-Tunya first seen by Europeans in 1855 it is now a popular tourist destination with around a million visitors each year the area round the falls is popular for adventure holidays and can easily be reached by bus and train

> Take care not to use commas to join separate sentences (see more on this on page 41).

....

....

....

....

....

....

....

....

Other ways of ending a sentence

Exclamation marks	• indicate strong feeling	Stop!
Question marks	• indicate a question	Where are you going?

Sometimes you need to punctuate combinations of words that are not full sentences. You probably just need a full stop, unless your words need emphasis or form a question.

Remember

Sometimes it's effective to write in incomplete sentences but you still have to include punctuation.

1. **Using full stops, commas, exclamation marks, question marks and capital letters, make sense of this email from a tourist to her friend.**

Hi Hanna,

Wow that was my first thought on seeing Mosi-oa-Tunya what a waterfall that was my immediate reaction to the highlight of my holiday in Africa am I really here amazing all that water all that noise who would have thought I would ever have seen such a glorious sight it was one of the most memorable moments of my life enough hope all well with you must rush Rachel

Using question marks and exclamation marks

Questions usually require question marks, but there are some exceptions:

- In indirect (or reported) speech a question mark is not followed by a capital letter if followed by *she asked*, *he said*, etc.
- In indirect (or reported) speech a question is not usually followed by a question mark.
- Indirect questions do **not** require question marks.

Notice that **rhetorical** or **loaded** questions need question marks. They are direct questions, even if they don't necessarily expect answers, or expect a particular answer. Isn't that right?

The same phrase can sometimes be punctuated in different ways:

The plane has already landed!

The plane has already landed.

The plane has already landed?

Think about how these examples differ. Notice how the tone of voice differs between these sentences. This will help you to decide which punctuation mark to use.

> **Remember**
> Don't overuse exclamation marks! They create the appearance that you are shouting and losing control of your expression. An exclamation mark can be used for extreme feelings or to make a command more urgent.

2. **Turn these direct questions into indirect questions.**

   a Have you got any qualifications to teach English?

   ....

   b Do you all understand how that program works?

   ....

   c Sharon, when will Steve arrive?

   ....

   d What will happen to them next?

   ....

   e How can we be sure that this is the right answer?

   ....

3. **In the email below, some of the exclamations are unnecessary and some of the question marks are in the wrong place. Improve the writing by changing the punctuation.**

   > The concert was just incredible! We heard all our favourite band's greatest hits! The performance just blew your mind away! Can you imagine what it is like to be surrounding by hundreds of screaming fans. I was asked to their next gig too?

Commas

Commas	• separate different elements of a sentence	When you go out, make sure you lock the door.
	• separate items in a list	She bought shoes, trousers and a hat.
	• are used before and often after words, phrases, clauses that are not essential to a sentence.	Sathnam, my oldest friend, has gone to Thailand for his holiday.

Commas can change the meaning of a sentence, so they need to be correctly placed.

In lists, make sure that you don't separate a combination of words where one adjective modifies another, for example:

The bright red dress was her favourite.

Commas can be used to separate a series of actions in a sentence, to make it easier to read:

She watched, waited, then pounced.

Sometimes you want to include something – an aside – that isn't absolutely essential:

He's not, I think, going to take his driving test until next year.

1. Add commas in these lists where needed.

 a He always takes pens compasses pencils rulers and correction fluid into exams.

 b She thinks he is stupid dull and unimaginative.

 c The boy reached the gate hopped over and continued down the path.

 d Although it was not expensive the dress looked fabulous.

2. Fill the gaps in these sentences with words from the box, using commas where needed. Use the clues to help you decide which word fits best.

> *pans   bowls   lively   passed   indeed   interesting   failed   knives   spoons   stylish*

 a (An aside) ...., only when we see the results will we know whether the students have (two verbs)..or gained scholarships.

 b Her writing was described as (three adjectives).. and ....

 c Any decent kitchen will have (four nouns) sharp................ wooden................ plastic mixing .... and lots of metal .... for the oven.

3. Read this extract and add commas where needed.

> As you probably already know in order to be fully fit you need to eat a balanced diet. Sweets chocolates crisps sugary drinks and cake though providing variety do not give you the vitamins minerals and dietary fibre that are essential to a busy healthy lifestyle. It is of course perfectly possible to live your life without eating meat. Indeed many people think that a fully vegetarian diet that contains beans pulses and cereals as well as a wide variety of the more obvious vegetables – carrots potatoes cabbage tomatoes etc. – is the best option. Whatever you choose to eat — whether you are vegetarian vegan or meat eating — the most important thing seems to be that you should eat in moderation and ensure that you consume nutritious tasty food from a wide variety of food groups each day.

4. Rewrite the extract below, correcting the punctuation. Some of the commas should be full stops; others are correct. You will need to add some capital letters too.

> Although I like hot weather, I don't like to lie in the sun, my brother does, when we were on holiday last summer he spent too much time by the pool this meant that I didn't get the opportunity to see all the monuments, museums and art galleries, it was a shame, as I had hoped to improve my knowledge of Indian, culture and history, I met some interesting people from all over the world, of course, however on the whole, the holiday was a bit disappointing.

....

....

....

....

....

....

....

....

....

....

....

Colons

Colons	• introduce an example	She was very clever: she passed all her exams first time.
	• introduce a list	You will need three things for this recipe: apples, sugar, lemon.
	• often introduce a quotation	He said: "I'll have to go."

Not all lists are introduced by a colon. You only need a colon if your sentence tells your reader that a list is coming up. This one is correct:

You must bring the following to school each day: compasses, pencils and pens.

This one can do without a colon.

You should bring compasses, pencils and pens to school each day.

1. Rewrite these sentences, using colons if they are needed.

a If you are going to India, you ought to see the Taj Mahal, The Red Fort, and New Delhi.

....

....

b It is easy to use a smartphone even my grandma knows how to text.

....

c Please bring at least one of the things from the following list a tent, a change of clothes and enough food to last 24 hours.

....

....

d She did very well in the national competition she won second prize.

....

e I went shopping and bought a kettle, a saucepan and a knife.

....

Semi-colons

Semi-colons	• are used between statements that are closely related in a sentence	Marika went out; her mother stayed at home to read a book.
	• are used instead of commas in complex lists where commas are also involved	She visited Venice, with its canals; Rome, to see the wonderful art; and she finished in Milan, home to her grandparents.

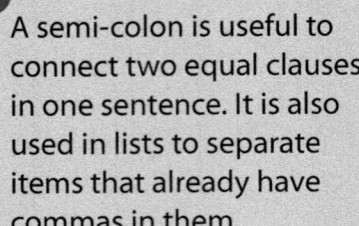

A semi-colon is useful to connect two equal clauses in one sentence. It is also used in lists to separate items that already have commas in them.

Linking thoughts

You can use the semi-colon at times where you are not sure whether a comma or a full stop is correct.

If you know that you have two equal clauses in a sentence, then you need something stronger than a comma to join them. Using only a comma is called a 'comma splice' and it is a big mistake. For example:

> There is no path, visitors must walk up the river bed.

This could be two sentences. A semi-colon relates the two parts and shows that they are aspects of the same topic:

> There is no path; visitors must walk up the river bed.

Similarly,

> The candidate failed to impress; he had plainly not prepared himself for the interview.

Each element of this sentence could stand on its own. It might be better to make this single sentence into two sentences. If the elements in a sentence are closely related, they can be joined with a conjunction (*and* or *but*), or a semi-colon.

1. **You could also use a colon in the sentence about the interview candidate because** ....

....

2. **Add semi-colons to the following sentences, where relevant.**

   a He loves maths she can't stand it.

   b Our school specialises in music and the arts the one down the road is more focused on sports.

   c We wanted to eat hamburgers and chips my mother had different ideas.

   d The winters in Canada are cold and long in Florida, however, they hardly even exist.

Sometimes you need to make the link between the two parts of a sentence even clearer. You do this by using words such as *therefore*, *nevertheless*, *however*, *moreover*, *consequently*, *otherwise* and *besides* after the semi-colon:

> For her birthday, she thinks she's going to the zoo; however, we
> know that something else is planned.

3. **Using some of the words listed above write six sentences that make use of the semi-colon followed by a joining word. You often need a comma after these words to help emphasise contrasts.**

....

....

....

....

....

....

Semi-colons and lists

Sometimes you need to use semi-colons because you have already had to use commas to add detail. For example:

> You will need the following: a small potato, sliced; two boiled eggs, cooled
> and peeled; carrots that are cleaned, washed and peeled; an onion, chopped.

Putting it all together

4. **Insert colons and semi-colons into this extract where they are needed.**

> He saw the shape of a giant towering above him it was Grendel's mother.
>
> She pinned him down she pulled a knife. This looked like the end Beowulf feared
>
> that it was. However, the knife was blunt Beowulf's armour was strong. He seized
>
> the sword with one stroke he swung round instantly, the monster was dead. He had
>
> displayed the courage of a true hero superhuman effort determination stronger
>
> than that of lesser men fearlessness in the face of almost certain death.

Hyphens

Hyphens	• are used to join words together to make compound words	The blue-eyed baby smiled.
	• make a group of words into an expression	The do-it-yourself man was a bit hit-and-miss with the paint.
	• link numbers that are written as more than one word	Ninety-nine balloons drifted past.
		The jug was three-quarters full.
	• help to avoid confusion when you add a prefix to a word	I'm going to re-cover my textbooks when I recover.

1. **Add the nine hyphens that are needed to this extract.**

> The half deaf lady was ninety four years old. Her good for nothing grandson never visited, except to take her to the end of term party. She usually arrived with home made jam in mis labelled jars. Without fail, the lady and her grandson were precisely twenty five minutes late.

2. **Add a hyphen where it is needed in each sentence.**
 a A walking stick is very useful in the hills.
 b "There is a man eating tiger outside," she cried.
 c Extra curricular activities are really important at our school.
 d He gets three monthly bank statements.
 e The one armed man guarded the bank vault.

3. **Now choose two of the sentences above and explain why the hyphen makes a difference.**

....

....

....

....

....

Dashes and brackets

Dashes	• are used singly or in pairs for an afterthought, an added example or explanation	Her journey – wildly exciting though it was – had to come to an end when the new school year began.
Brackets	• provide an added example or explanation • can be used (like dashes) to put in an additional comment or afterthought	Kafka (born 1883) mainly wrote novels. We had to wait for an hour before we could buy tickets (there was a very long queue).

1. **Add a single dash or pair of dashes to each of these sentences to make it easier to understand.**

   a The whole holiday the tickets, the airport, the hotel, the food was a disaster.

   b There is something I need to tell you it won't be a surprise.

   c We watched a film quite entertaining if I remember rightly on the first night of the holiday.

   d Intelligence, good humour, sporting ability all of these are typical of my sister's friends.

2. **Add brackets where they are needed in each of these sentences.**

   a Please ask the secretary room 64 if you need an application form.

   b You need to add two tablespoons 40 grams of honey.

   c There is more on this in Chapter 4 pages 19–20.

   d London in Ontario is home to a number of universities.

   e We had bought tickets to the show in advance they were very hard to get rather than just turning up on the night.

As you will have noticed, sometimes brackets and pairs of dashes can be used interchangeably – it's a matter of taste – for asides. Dashes are less formal, perhaps, and used more for the sorts of aside that you might include when talking to someone.

Skillcheck

If you know all the rules given so far in this chapter, you will have
no difficulty with the following.

**1. Two of these sentences are wrongly punctuated. Which ones are they? Why is the
punctuation wrong?**

   a Your interview is at 11a.m. tomorrow, it is preceded by a briefing session.

   b Your interview is at 11a.m. tomorrow; it is preceded by a briefing session.

   c Your interview is at 11a.m. tomorrow — it is preceded by a briefing session.

   d Your interview is at 11a.m. tomorrow, but it is preceded by a briefing session.

   e Your interview is at 11a.m. tomorrow; however, it is preceded by a briefing session.

   f Your interview is at 11a.m. tomorrow, however, it is preceded by a briefing session.

   Sentence .... is incorrect because...

   ....

   Sentence .... is incorrect because...

   ....

2. Now explain why the other four sentences are correct and the differences in their meanings.

....

....

....

....

....

....

....

....

....

....

Apostrophes

Apostrophes	• show possession	Ahmina's bag is heavy.
	• show contraction	I can't come tomorrow.

The apostrophe is often misused, but learning where it should appear isn't as hard as it might seem at first.

Possession

Here are three rules about possession.

- **If something belongs to someone or something, you need an apostrophe:**

    This is the boy's jacket.

- **If the possessor is plural, you add the apostrophe after the s:**

    This is the students' homework.

- **If the possessor is singular and the word ends with an *s*, the apostrophe goes after the first *s*.** You can add a second if you wish.

    This is a list of Dickens's novels.

> A common error is to put an apostrophe at the end of a noun by accident. For example:
>
> Potatoe's sold here or Toilet's.
>
> Make sure you don't make this mistake!

1. **Refer to the three rules above. Rewrite these sentence so that an apostrophe is needed in each sentence and add the apostrophe in the right place.**

    a The toys of the children were lying all over the floor.

    ....

    b The clothes belonging to Rakesh were all in a pile near the door.

    ....

    c The day room belonging to the teachers was always packed at recess.

    ....

    d The legs belonging to the table were wobbly.

    ....

    e In the time of two weeks, my holiday starts.

    ....

    f In the time of one month, my sister is expecting a baby.

    ....

2. Look at the four phrases below. How many girls are there? How many friends?
Write either '1' or '2 or more' in each space.

a the girl's friend's bag.

Girls = ...   Friends = ...

b the girls' friends' bag.

Girls = ...   Friends = ...

c the girl's friends' bag.

Girls = ...   Friends = ...

d the girls' friend's bag.

Girls = ...   Friends = ...

Contraction

**Be careful not to confuse an apostrophe that shows possession
with one that shows contraction:**

I'd just come out of the dentist's when I heard my phone ring. I had to
tell Sam's mother that I couldn't come to the party tonight.

1. **Write out this extract, putting in contraction apostrophes
where possible.**

I will not be able to come to the party. I cannot even get out of bed
just now because I am ill. I have not been out for some days. You can
tell me what has been happening at school. I would bet that no one is
doing any work because it will soon be the holidays. I cannot imagine
that I will be back before the break. You had better give my best
wishes to everyone. Do not forget that you are invited to my birthday
party next month.

....

....

....

....

....

....

2. **Decide if the following sentences use apostrophes correctly. If the sentence is incorrect, rewrite the sentence correctly.**

a Im going to cook carrots' this evening.

....

....

b Theres nothing that you can do about the situation. He will never change hi's mind.

....

....

c The women's shoe's are over there.

....

....

d Hell never go there again — it's a terrible place.

....

....

e I can't hear you.

....

f Priyas homework is always perfect.

....

g I couldn't come because Ive been busy.

....

h Whos coming to town with me?

....

i Whose coat is this?

....

j Wed love to come to the party.

....

Never use an apostrophe in the word *its* if you mean 'belonging to it'. *It's* means *it is*, and the apostrophe is here to demonstrate contraction. *Its* is a possessive pronoun like *his*. If you are in doubt, decide you will never use the apostrophe in this situation, so that you will always have to decide between *its* and *it is*.

Punctuation of speech

Quotation marks	• show that someone is speaking • are used for titles of poems, works of art, films and television programmes.	"Auckland is very pleasant," he said. 'The Eagle' by Tennyson

- Actual words spoken by someone are surrounded by either single or double quotation marks:

    "Is this the way to the airport?" asked Raghu.

- The first word spoken has a capital letter, even if it comes in the middle of a sentence:

    Raghu asked, "Is this the way to the airport?"

- Punctuation marks that are part of what is said go inside the quotation marks. (See the question marks in the two examples above.)

- When someone else starts to speak, you start a new paragraph, and usually this is indented from the left margin:

    "Your dinner is ready," she said. He put down the paper that he had been reading and quickly got to his feet.

    "Just coming," he replied.

- Once you have started using (either double or single) quotation marks you must stick with your choice.

- If words are quoted within spoken words, you must use double quotation marks if single ones are normally used, or single ones if double ones are normally used. Here is an example of words quoted within speech that has been given single quotation marks.

    'He asked, "Have you bought the tickets?" and I replied that they were in my bag,' she said.

    Here is how the example should appear if you are using single quotation marks for speech within double quotation marks:

    "He asked, 'Have you bought the tickets?' and I replied that they were in my bag," she said.

More on quotation marks

You should also use quotation marks (either single or double) when:

- you write words or phrases directly quoted from something else
- you need to draw attention to words that are being used in a special sense
- you quote a title of a poem, a television programme, a film, a work or art or a section of a book or play.

Here's an example: 'To be or not to be' is a famous line from Shakespeare's *Hamlet*.

> Full titles of books or plays should appear in italics. If you are writing these yourself by hand, use quotation marks around them instead. (If you are using a word processor, you will be able to use italics.)

1. **Insert quotation marks in the correct places in these sentences.**

a Is curiouser really a proper word?

b I'll be back is a famous line from the film The Terminator.

c He always watches the programme Africa on Thursdays.

d She wanted to know if he had visited the Chhatrapati Shivaji railway terminus in Mumbai on his journey, as it was used as a setting in Slumdog Millionaire.

e I can't remember which of Shakespeare's plays includes the speech To be or not to be.

f Did you go to the Boston Red Sox game yesterday?

If you need to avoid confusion between speech and quotation, use single quotation marks for one, and double quotation marks for the other. For example: 'I'm going to see "The Hobbit" this afternoon,' he said.

2. **Rewrite this discussion between friends. Add the correct punctuation and start a new paragraph if you think you need one.**

Did you see the first episode of My Brilliant Friend last night? he asked. No, she replied, My parents wanted me to go and see some awful kids film called Fishy. Yes, he replied, I don't much like childrens films these days, though I did enjoy Islands of Adventure. I really like the song Sing It Loud. You're joking, she said, Id thought of you more as a suspense film fan.

....

....

....

....

....

....

1. Rewrite the passage below as follows:

- Use capital letters where they are needed.
- Indent the first line when someone starts speaking.
- Add the correct speech punctuation.
- You will need some contraction apostrophes too.

Tell us a story! said the March Hare Yes please do! pleaded Alice and be quick about it added the Hatter or youll be asleep before its done once upon a time there were three little sisters the Doormouse began in a great hurry and their names were Elsie, Lacie and Tillie and they lived in the bottom of a well What did they live on said Alice who always took a great interest in questions of eating and drinking they lived on treacle said the Dormouse after thinking a minute or two they couldnt have done that you know Alice gently remarked theyd have been ill so they were, said the Dormouse very ill.

From *Alice's Adventures in Wonderland* by Lewis Carroll.

Direct and reported speech

Sometimes you need to report what someone has said. Look at this example:

> "I am leaving my job at the end of term," said the teacher.

In reported speech it becomes:

> The teacher said that she was leaving her job at the end of term.

This is what you need to do to convert direct speech to reported speech.

- You need to change the word order, so that the speaker is identified near the beginning of the sentence.

- You need to make sure that pronouns are changed. For example, *I* becomes *she* in the sentence above.

- You need to change possessive adjectives. For example, *my* becomes *her* in the sentence above.

- You need to link the speaker to what is said, using a word such as *that*.

- You need to change the present tense to the past, as you are reporting what *was* said. If parts of the direct speech are already in the past tense, you need to use the distant past tense too. For example, if the speech contains *she ate* you need to change it to *she had eaten*:

> "She ate the mildly flavoured chicken instead of the spicy prawn option," the waiter told the chef.

> The waiter told the chef that the girl had eaten the mildly flavoured chicken instead of the spicy prawn option.

- As in the example above, you may need to add some words to improve the clarity or the flow of the writing.

Indirect or reported speech, like the passive voice, is useful for reported incidents. Instead of the drama of dialogue, indirect speech provides a formal record, which is placed in the past tense.

The present tense changes to the past tense, and the perfect tense to the distant past. The word order may also change.

Indirect speech is used in a report, when an accurate record of what was said is needed. It is also used in a story where the narrator is looking back and describing her or his thoughts and feelings by reporting what was said.

1. **Write the correct form of the verbs in these sentences.**

    a Fran (say) .... she would be there at 4 o'clock.

    b Mr Singh claimed that they (cheat) .... in the test.

    c The Prime Minister insisted that the final decision (make) ....

2. **Convert these examples of direct speech into indirect speech. You need to take out the punctuation and put everything into the past tense.**

    a "I'll make sure I have the right books with me next time," said Seun.

    ....

    b Pam insisted, "Keep away from the edge of the platform, John!"

    ....

    c "It's Mary's turn to do the chores today," claimed Paul.

    ....

    d "We will deliver the goods on time," promised the man at the warehouse.

    ....

    e "I didn't do it!" shouted out the prisoner in the dock.

    ....

3. **In your notebook, convert the indirect speech back into dialogue. You may need to revise the rules for punctuating direct speech (see page 52). Change the passive voice back to the active.**

> The committee were told by Amar that he would ensure everyone had early notice of the date for the fundraising party. Jules said the date needed to be fixed quickly so they could advertise on the website. Amar explained that he still needed to confirm the availability of the hall. As chairman, James suggested they work out catering arrangements and fundraising events. Jane thought the best way to deal with food was for everyone to bring one item that they had cooked or prepared, as this would be much cheaper than bringing in caterers. The others agreed this would be best.

....

....

....

....

....

4. Write out this extract again changing direct speech into reported speech. Check that your version has quotation marks (but not speech marks) and apostrophes of possession and contraction where they are needed.

> Did you see the first episode of My Brilliant Friend last night? he asked. No, she replied, My parents wanted me to go and see some awful kids film called Fishy instead. Yes, he replied, I don't much like childrens films these days, though I did enjoy Islands of Adventure. I really like the song Sing It Loud. You're joking, she said, Id thought of you more as a suspense film fan.

....

....

....

....

Editing your writing

Spelling and word processing

In this grammar guide it is not possible to explore all the rules of English spelling (and they differ across the world). One important point is that you can never assume that your spell checker will do the spelling for you. A spell checker is useful in finding any words that are obviously wrongly spelt. However, as you have learnt, words that mean quite different things can have very similar spellings. A spell checker will not be able to find places in your writing where you have used the wrong word.

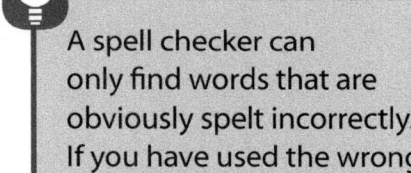

A spell checker can only find words that are obviously spelt incorrectly. If you have used the wrong word, the spell checker won't notice.

1. In places in these sentences you are given a choice of words to use. Underline the word that is correctly used in the sentence.

a He wanted to *proof/prove* that he hadn't stolen the money.

b No matter how hard you *practice/practise*, you will never play the guitar well.

c The very cold weather was particularly *seasonal/seasonable* that year, as it came at Christmas in New York.

d The appetiser always *precedes/proceeds* the main course.

e The children returned to their *respectable/respectful/respective* bedrooms.

f She pushed the trolley up the supermarket *isle/aisle*.

g He kept his boat in the *creak/creek*.

h She *heard/herd* the *herd/heard* returning to the barn.

i They put their clothes on *hangars/hangers* in the wardrobe.

j By going to the gym, he hoped to develop more *mussels/muscles*.

k She showed a real *flare/flair* for drawing.

l Born in India, with one American parent, she has *dual/duel* nationality.

2. Write out a corrected version of this rhyme.

Eye halve a spelling chequer
It came with my pea sea
It plainly marques four my revue
Miss steaks eye kin knot sea.

Eye strike a key and type a word
And weight four it two say
Weather eye am wrong oar write
It shows me strait a weigh.

As soon as a mist ache is maid
It nose bee fore two long
And eye can put the error rite
Its rare lea ever wrong.

Eye have run this poem threw it
I am shore your pleased two no
Its letter perfect awl the weigh
My chequer tolled me sew.

—Sauce unknown

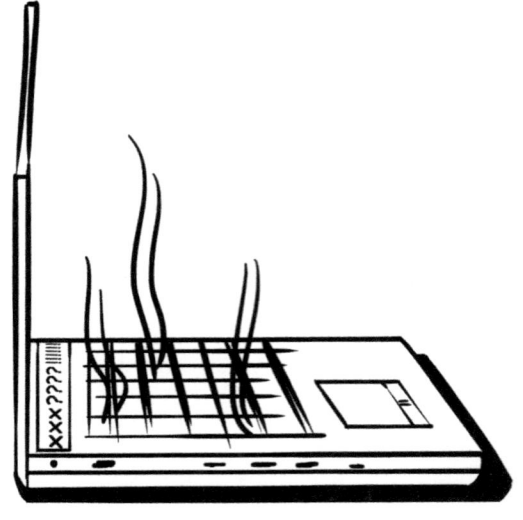

....

....

....

....

....

....

....

....

....

....

....

....

....

....

Common errors

In many cases when speaking and writing English, correctness is a matter of taste. However, there are some things that you should try to avoid, as they seem particularly likely to cause offence. Here are some examples.

Me and ***I*:** If you are going somewhere you say "I am going out." The presence of someone else makes no difference, so you need to say "Isla and I are going out." It is fine to say "between you and me"; "between you and I" is not acceptable.

Myself and ***me*:** *Myself* is an emphatic word, not a replacement for *me*. "I did it myself" is fine; "he gave it to myself yesterday" is not acceptable.

Fewer and ***less*:** *Fewer* is used for objects considered as a collection of individual items, for example: There are fewer cars on the road because of the price of fuel.

Less is used with abstract nouns and objects considered as a mass, for example: There is less room in the new car than in the old one.

Amount and ***number*:** Use amount when you think of an object that is one thing made up of many parts, for example: He always puts a large amount of sugar on his cereal. Use number when you refer to a collection of individual objects, for example: She owns a large number of pens.

***Double negatives*:** Think carefully about how many *not* words there are in a sentence. They can end up cancelling each other out, for example: She didn't do nothing to help in fact means she did do something to help.

***Like*:** Although it is used in conversation, you should only use *like* in writing if you are expressing a positive opinion, for example: I like ice cream; or when you are comparing something with something else, for example:

> Dolphins are like whales in that they are marine mammals.

In this final example, the word like is not necessary:

> She looks like a million dollars in her elaborate costume.

The following sentence would be equally correct:

> She looks a million dollars.

1. Tick any sentences that are correct. If the sentence is incorrect, cross out the word that is wrongly used and write the correct word in the space at the end of each sentence.

a Jasbir and myself went out to town on Saturday. .... ☐

b There was a large amount of food laid out in the kitchen before the guests arrived.

.... ☐

c There were many less people there by the end of the day than there had been
at the beginning. .... ☐

d She and I had been going to art classes for six months before she gave up. .... ☐

e You need to make less mistakes with your homework. .... ☐

f Between you and I, she needs to improve her work if she wants to go to college. .... ☐

g I didn't do nothing to break the window. .... ☐

h We're like just waiting to go away. We really like visiting the countryside. .... ☐

Checking your work and proofreading

An important element of writing is the checking stage when you
make sure that everything is correct and flows properly.

Look at the extract below. If you have paid attention to everything
you have read so far in this book, you will have no difficulty writing
it out again without mistakes. There are four distinct sections.
Each should be a separate paragraph.

> **Remember**
>
> Use a dictionary to look up
> the definitions of words you
> are not sure of.

My First Car

for years i have been driving an old used car with a lot of milage I hate it it gets me where I knead to
go but Im tired of fixing it's leeks and broken part's all the time It annoys me every time I need to take
it to the mechanics at the garage. Even when they takes care of everything i know i'll just end up going
back shortly with some new problem. Finally I have decided that even though I cant afford it I need to
to buy a new car. Unfortunately I have a problem. I have no idea what car to get. Do i want something
big? Do I want something fast! Something economical. I have so many choices that I don't even know
where to begins.

'Im not sure if I will be able to make a decision on my own'; As I said I don't have a lot of money
either, so I will probably have less options. After I did some re-search, I decided I would need some
expert advice: on friday I went to a local dealership to check out some new modals. I talked to the
salesperson, and listened carfully. Her honesty and professionalism was really impressive. She had a lot
of very helpful suggestions and she showed myself some some currant models from a limited amount
of affordable choices. I finaly decided which one I wanted. After a long discusion.

Writing a suspense story

Stories or myths involving suspense require imagination and the ability to create anxiety or fear about what might happen next. The most important person to consider is your reader. The reader needs to feel the tension and suspense and needs to identify with the situation and the characters.

Discuss these points with a partner.

- What kind of story do you and your friends like?
- Who are your friends' favourite heroes?
- What kind of monsters do these heroes need to fight or what problems do they overcome?

Begin by considering location and characters.

The location needs to have an element of danger or risk, such as an abandoned house, a tunnel or cave, a cliff top. Include two or three characters in your story. They must be characters that you (and your reader) can identify with. They could have some unusual abilities but if they are unable to be scared by the situation, the reader won't be scared either.

Next, consider viewpoint: who is going to tell the story? You can use first person or third person narration. If you use third person, giving the thoughts and feelings of one main character gives your reader someone to identify with.

Your characters will need to face a problem or fright – then overcome it! Most stories of this kind follow a sequence consisting of:

- a problem
- a cliff-hanger or dilemma
- a climax
- a resolution (the problem is overcome).

1. **Using bullet points, write the events of your story in order.**

2. **Decide if the sequence would be improved by putting the cliff-hanger first and then explaining how you got there. If so, write your bullets again in the new order.**

Vocabulary will also be important. You need vivid verbs that bring the tension to life. You have also learnt that variety is the key to good sentences and sentences need to be structured around different forms of punctuation.

Over to you

Choose one scenario below to write a story. Use the checklists to plan, check and then assess your writing.

1. Write a story about a dangerous task your hero has to perform.
2. Use this sentence to begin a story: 'The mill had been abandoned for many years…'.
3. Write a story with the title 'Out in the dark'.
4. Write a story with the title 'An unexpected visitor'.

Planning your writing

Describe the location.	
Who are the characters and whose viewpoint do we share?	
What is the problem or dilemma?	
What are the characters' thoughts and feelings?	
What will make the climax tense and exciting? Add time pressure.	
How will the characters solve the problem and resolve the tension?	

Checking your writing

Check your writing against this list. Improve your work as needed until you can tick each item.

Have you used interesting adjectives for description?	
Are your characters lively and contrasting? Have you used dialogue correctly?	
Are your paragraphs short and well-structured?	
Have you included your main character's thoughts (using **similes** and **metaphors**)?	
Have you used short sentences and vivid verbs?	
Have you provided a clear explanation and a sense of relief at the end?	

Assessing your writing

Assess your work based on these questions. Note any areas you need to improve.

What are the strengths and weaknesses of your writing and its effect on the reader?	
Which is your most convincing character and why?	
Can you improve the vocabulary you use for effect?	
Can you improve the accuracy of your writing and the variety of your sentences?	

Writing a newspaper report

Newspaper reports need to hold readers' attention. We like to know the news, but may not have time for too much detail. News articles are structured with a first level which introduces the subject and the main point. Most of the newspaper's readers will read this level. Not all of them will continue reading through further levels of the article, but the stages to these levels can help to answer these questions: What? Who? When? Where? How? Why?

Some newspaper articles are reports, which place emphasis on facts. Other articles are features, which present opinions. To see some examples, look at the articles opposite the editorial in a newspaper (known as 'op-eds'), or look at the links to features and opinion pieces that follow a news report online.

Newspaper reporting sometimes gets a reputation for bias. To write a good newspaper report, it is important to get your facts right, and clearly distinguish between facts and opinions. Don't present your own opinion; present the opinions of others, giving their names and using quotation marks. As a reporter, it is your job to ask the questions, and present other people's answers.

You can practise this skill by learning how to interview.

> In pairs, interview a partner who takes the role of someone with strong opinions about a topic you are both interested in. Write questions that will help the partner to present his or her opinions, rather than present your point of view.

Use the following points as you train to become a news reporter:

- Remember to get the reader's attention, first through headlines, opening paragraph, picture and caption.
- A little hyperbole will make your writing more exciting: but keep to the facts!
- For variety, use two different ways of communicating opinions: direct and reported speech.
- Journalists often aim to give stories human interest. Give the ages of the people you have interviewed and perhaps roughly where they live: in local news, this helps readers to identify with them.
- Journalists talk about 'giving stories colour'. Give colour to your descriptions by using adverbs.
- Make sure you also have paragraphs that present and explain the facts: this is important in any report. Explain what has just happened and then why it matters.

Over to you

Choose one scenario below to write a news report. Use the checklists to plan, check and then assess your writing.

1. A new school is being opened in your neighbourhood and will have a particular specialism that makes it different from existing schools.

2. A local sports person has won a national trophy.

3. Your community is making a bid for much-needed new facilities. What choices will people have to make?

4. Your school is sponsoring a foreign development project. Write a report about your school's involvement in the project.

Planning your writing

Write a headline to attract attention and an exciting first paragraph.	
Give details of a suitable picture and caption.	
Human interest: describe the people involved. Add quotations.	
Explanation: give more detail about what happened when and where. Get the facts right.	
Analysis: explain how the event happened and what can be done about it. Use quotations for opinions.	

Checking your writing

Check your writing against this list. Improve your work as needed until you can tick each item.

Is the opening clear and straightforward; have you used short sentences?	
Have you written interesting descriptions of places and people?	
Have you correctly used direct speech (for quotations) and indirect speech (for reported comments)?	
Have you separated facts and opinions?	
Have you used interesting adverbs to add colour?	
Have you added detail and explanation to keep the reader's attention?	

Assessing your writing

Assess your work based on these questions. Note any areas you need to improve.

What are the strengths and weaknesses of your report's structure?	
Which is your most interesting paragraph and why?	
Can you improve the vocabulary you use to present facts accurately and interestingly?	
Can you improve the accuracy of your punctuation, especially of direct speech?	
What have you done to separate facts from opinions?	

Writing a description of a journey

Travel writing is a very popular genre. Description of travel needs to be based on real life, and its authority comes from personal experience. Human interest means that we take an interest in people who have had unusual experiences and who can communicate them in an exciting way.

Take care not to confuse writing a description of a journey with writing a story. You should be the first person narrator of travel writing and you should describe something that has happened to you. You are allowed to 'improve' the experience; for example, you could invent or extend conversations with other travellers to make the dialogue more interesting. The trick is to make sure it always sounds as if what you are describing did really happen.

Journeys make for well-structured writing: they have a beginning, a middle and an end. The challenge is to make them interesting and unpredictable. Selection is important; so is variety. Look out for unusual details, language and encounters with places or people.

Don't feel you need to describe everything; it's better to go into more detail about what is most interesting to your reader. Describe characters who are with you on the journey, or who you meet along the way and give them interesting dialogue. Make sure you have defined the time frame and the end point. You don't need to describe the entire journey. How will you structure the time between the start and the end? You could use chronology, base your writing on the five senses, or use other ways to focus the reader's attention on detail.

Your writing will be assessed for its use of language as well as its structure and content. Adjectives are clearly important in descriptive writing, but also consider the following.

- What other language features are important?
- Why are similes especially effective in this genre and what is their effect on the reader?
- When would you use short sentences for effect?
- When are longer sentences more appropriate?
- Why might you use the passive as well as the active voice?
- How will you make sure your writing communicates movement?

Over to you

Choose one scenario below to write a piece of travel writing. Use the checklists to plan, check and then assess your writing.

1. Describe your journey to your school or college.

2. Describe the ways in which you made a long journey interesting.

3. Describe your journey to an event you had been looking forward to for a long time.

4. Describe your arrival in a place very different from anywhere you had ever been before.

Planning your writing

Setting the scene: write a paragraph that explains where you start from and why.	
Going into detail: record what you notice on your journey.	
Ensuring human interest: describe interesting people and what they have to say.	
Conveying movement: make sure your journey has a structure and keeps moving on. What do you see? What do you feel?	
Reaching your destination: describe the journey's end point and your thoughts and feelings when you get there.	

Checking your writing

Check your writing against this list. Improve your work as needed until you can tick each item.

Is the opening clear and interesting: have you managed to engage your reader?	
Is the description of places and people unusual: have you made a powerful choice of adjectives and adverbs?	
Is there a variety of paragraphs and sentences: are there long ones for description or information and short ones for feelings?	
Is punctuation accurate and effective: e.g. have you used a rhetorical question to involve your reader and an exclamation mark to express your feeling? (One is enough!)	
Have you used similes to help your readers to form their own picture of the scene?	
Does the language you use appeal to the senses?	
Is the end point strong: does your writing reach a destination and not just stop?	

Assessing your writing

Assess your work based on these questions. Note any areas you need to improve.

What are the strengths and weaknesses of your personal viewpoint in this task?	
Which was your best description and what made it work well?	
How can you improve the sequence of descriptions and paragraphs?	
Did you punctuate long sentences accurately?	

Writing a scene from a play

Writing a playscript is fun. You are freed up from some of the conventions of more formal writing, because your script needs to sound like authentic dialogue – comments that characters would really make to each other. There is no need to write in paragraphs and you simply need to identify the speaker of the lines in the margin. However, your writing needs to be carefully structured: you must tell a lot of story without too many words. The words have to fit the characters. Stage directions are also important: you need to give guidance so that other people can perform your script, describing the setting and props, and any actions that need to be performed.

The best way to write a script is in collaboration with those who are going to act it. You might be going to act in the play, or you might want to direct the play. The director watches and guides the actors to make sure that they are getting the drama across to the **audience** (and can be seen by them). It's very hard to direct and act in the same play, or to write and play a large part in a play.

Who will play which part? Casting is crucial. Think about your group of actors and what will work for them.

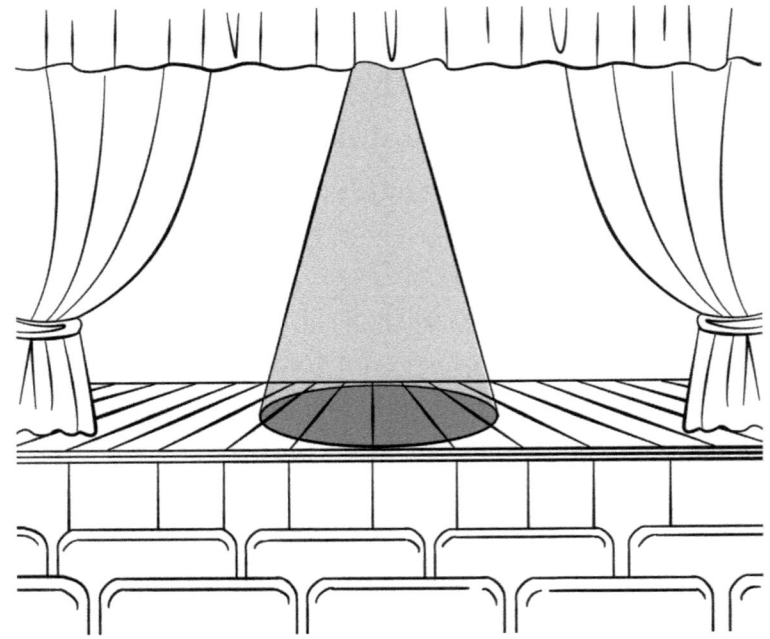

Scenic form means thinking about who we meet, what happens between them, and what the consequences will be. Audiences may find it difficult if they are introduced to several characters at once. Present only two characters at first, then bring in a third, and perhaps a fourth, character. Think about *where* as well as *when* entrances and exits will take place. Details will need to be included in the stage directions.

Duologues are the building blocks of drama: they introduce two characters through dialogue. Think about the effectiveness of a monologue, when a character communicates his or her thoughts to an audience directly.

Drama is about movement. Characters need to move and develop, and an audience needs to be moved emotionally. Tension, suspense and climax are also important in this genre.

The best way to learn about drama is to act it out, and the second best way is to write it yourself. Make sure you have chances to do both, so that you understand how actors will present your writing.

Over to you

Choose one scenario below to write a playscript. Use the checklists to plan, check and then assess your writing.

1. One character has an important ticket or other piece of paper. At a key moment in the play, he or she will rip it up.

2. A pair of twins have grown up without knowing of the other's existence. What happens next?

3. A prank or bet which should have been funny goes badly wrong.

4. You are stranded on a desert island with people you don't trust.

Planning your writing

Opening: make sure it is clear who is who. Introduce two contrasting characters.	
Develop the situation: bring in one or two new characters, perhaps someone with some news or someone who provokes conflict.	
Develop conflict and a problem. Make sure the problem is explained.	
Develop tension by leaving the audience uncertain, or develop a situation where members of the audience know things the characters don't know.	
Make sure there is an exciting climax, with all the characters on stage at the end. (They can be alive or dead!)	

Checking your writing

Check your writing against this list. Improve your work as needed until you can tick each item.

Check your stage directions: is it clear who is on stage and where actors enter and exit?	
Is it always clear who is speaking about whom? Check pronouns very carefully.	
Have you varied the length of speeches and sentences: used long ones for explanations or stories and short ones to express emotions in a punchy way?	
Exclamation marks can be very effective – but don't overuse them!	
Do your stage directions use adverbs to describe how actors should speak their lines?	
Does the language you use match each character? Does it sound natural?	

Assessing your writing

Assess your work based on these questions. Note any areas you need to improve.

How did you make it clear that this was a drama text?	
Which were your best and most dramatic lines and why?	
How successful were you in developing the situation?	
Where did you use sentence structures for effect and how?	

Writing a science fiction story

As the name suggests, science fiction tells a story but needs to sound as if it is real. You need some scientific knowledge to support this. Take an interesting fact or possibility and project it into the future. What would be the consequences of new forms of technology? What are the possibilities of genetic engineering or other medical developments? Many stories are based on the consequences of cloning or our use of robots and replicants.

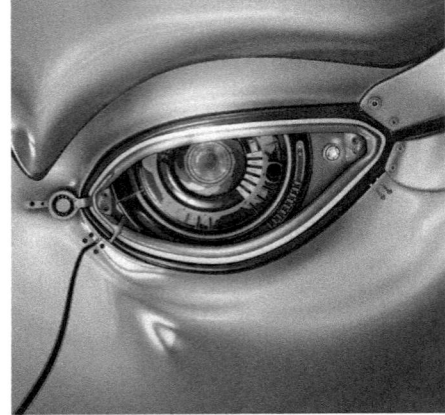

Choose a topic you know something about, do some research and then use your imagination. Finding out some science facts first will make your science fiction better. Once you have done some research, discuss with a partner how different our world will be in 50 years' time.

Voyages through time are a favourite way of introducing science fiction. To travel to a different time period or planetary system you will need a portal, or gateway. This can be an apparently ordinary object, such as a wardrobe, which transports you to another place, a time machine of some kind or simply a window into a different world.

Over to you

Two travellers find a portal that takes them into a very different world. They have a task to perform there! Choose one or two of the following items to include in a science fiction story. Use the checklists to plan, check and then assess your writing.

1. Robots
2. Aliens
3. Different forms of technology
4. The possibility of time travel (forwards or backwards).

Planning your writing

Opening (two or three paragraphs): introduce your two travellers. How did they find the portal? What is it like to go through it and what do they see?	
Develop your story through an encounter with someone who gives the travellers a task. Include a dialogue. The conversation should begin to reveal more about the world your travellers have discovered.	

Describe conflicts that arise and problems that are solved as the travellers meet enemies and helpers on their journey.	
Develop tension by putting the travellers under time pressure to complete an important task or mission.	
After the climactic moment, how are your travellers going to get back to their world?	

Checking your writing

Check your writing against this list. Improve your work as needed until you can tick each item.

Is your writing clear, with a logical sequence of events leading to a climax and resolution (return)?	
Have you used a mixture of formal (scientific) language for explanations and informal language for dialogue?	
Have you used interesting subject-specific vocabulary? Have you checked the spelling of unusual words and ensured that you have used them correctly and so that their meaning is clear?	
Have you used sentence structure to build up tension: longer sentences for description and explanation and short sentences for urgency and action?	
Have you made sure your characters sound different from each other through choice of words and form of expression?	
Have you used adjectives and alliteration to make your descriptions memorable and effective?	

Assessing your writing

Assess your work based on these questions. Note any areas you need to improve.

Did a writing frame make your story structured and original?	
How successful were you in establishing character and setting?	
How did plot twists and complications help to develop your story?	
Where did you use scientific facts and vocabulary to make your story less fantastical?	
Did you manage to sustain your choice of tenses and narrative viewpoint all the way through your story?	
Were you pleased with the way your story ended? Would you make changes to your plan next time?	

Writing a biography

Writing a biography involves mastering a range of facts about an interesting person and communicating them in an organised and original way. If you are writing a biography about a famous person, it will be easy to find out bare facts on the Internet. You need to think about how to transform these bare facts into an interesting story. From this story, readers should find things out, map the ways characters develop and change, and find answers to their questions about the subject of the biography.

Most biographies are structured around chronology, but it might be a good idea to begin by thinking of some questions you would like your biography to answer. What would you like to find out about your subject? For example, what were the early influences on the person? What experiences changed your subject's life? What effect did he or she have on others? How can you sum up your subject's achievements? (If it is possible to interview the person, plan to ask questions such as these.) The answers will help to give your writing structure.

Over to you

Choose one subject below to write a biography. Use the checklists to plan, check and then assess your writing.

1. An family member more than 20 years older than you.
2. A famous historical figure who made a difference to our world.
3. A person still alive today who you think is a good role model.
4. Someone famous for a particular skill or invention.

Planning your writing

Opening: introduce your subject by describing what most people think about the person today and by introducing some questions you would like to answer.	
Use description to capture your subject's childhood and school life.	
Develop your writing by going into detail about a particular incident that was important for your subject's later life.	
Describe the significance of the most important thing your subject did. Use quotations from other people to support the importance of this achievement.	

Reflect on your subject's formative influences, what the person achieved and why that mattered. Give answers to the questions you wanted to answer.	

Checking your writing

Check your writing against this list. Improve your work as needed until you can tick each item.

Is the chronology clear and balanced? Have you explained early influences, formative experiences and great achievements?	
Have you made your descriptive writing vivid, in order to recreate the places and experience that influenced your subject's life?	
Did you ask interesting questions about your subject – and answer them?	
Have you used subject-specific vocabulary that fits the person's interests and achievements? Have you explained any difficult vocabulary or concepts?	
Have you used short topic sentences to introduce your paragraphs and longer sentences for descriptions or explanations? Have you used connectives to introduce and link paragraphs?	
Have you used formal vocabulary appropriate to your subject? Have you use more informal language in quotations so that they sound more like speech?	

Assessing your writing

Assess your work based on these questions. Note any areas you need to improve.

Did you achieve a balanced chronology, giving the right weight to different parts of your subject's life?	
What was the most successful story or anecdote you told about your subject?	
Where did you manage to introduce opinions as well as facts about your subject?	
Did you sustain a formal vocabulary throughout your story, or are there areas where this can be improved?	
Where did you most successfully use language to achieve an effect and what did you learn from this?	
Did you manage to answer all the questions you had about your subject by the end? Do you think you kept your reader interested?	

Writing a persuasive article

There is a clear difference between a news report, which presents the facts, and a persuasive article, which concentrates on opinions. Writing blogs, commentaries and 'op-eds' are various ways in which writers post their opinions about issues, presenting their own arguments in a way that is clearly biased. The aim is to persuade readers to share the writer's opinions.

You will need facts to support your opinions. You should also collect facts that might be used by your opponents. Use these facts for counter-arguments to 'rebut' your opponents' views.

Your argument will be more persuasive if it has balance and is not just a biased rant. Not only should you do research to ensure that evidence supports your opinions, but you should look at what the other side might say. Evaluate opponents' arguments and point out weaknesses. This will gain you much higher marks.

Use technical vocabulary (jargon) to show your expertise, but make sure you also explain things in ways anyone can understand. A simile or comparison can help to achieve this.

Remember throughout your article that you must involve your readers and persuade them to share your views. Language features are essential. Use them for a purpose. Here are some examples.

- **Rhetorical questions** help you to engage readers' interest and get them thinking.
- The rule of three (or using a tricolon) groups ideas together in a memorable way.
- Alliteration can be used to present your arguments in memorable ways.
- Antithesis helps you to contrast opinions, facts and arguments.
- Emotive language engages your readers' feelings.
- Modal verbs give your readers directions.
- Imperatives add urgency to your arguments – and urge your readers to take action. You should end a persuasive piece by encouraging your readers to do something.

Over to you

Choose one subject below to write a persuasive article. Use the checklists to plan, check and then assess your writing.

1. Present arguments in favour of an unpopular food and state its advantages.
2. Present an argument for why a particular film should be seen or a particular book should be read.
3. Persuade your readers of ways in which their environment can be improved.
4. Persuade your readers to do something to help a charitable cause.

Planning your writing

Opening: introduce your topic clearly.	
Develop your opinions through presenting important facts.	
Counter the views of opponents by explaining why they are wrong.	
Use persuasive and emotive features of language to advise your readers what they should do.	
End with a climax. Why is the issue you are writing about so important and what should your readers do now?	

Checking your writing

Check your writing against this list. Improve your work as needed until you can tick each item.

Have you addressed and involved your readers from the beginning?	
Have you used jargon and facts that show readers your mastery of the subject?	
Do your counter-arguments convincingly rebut those who might oppose your views?	
Do sentences present your views clearly and informally? Have you used modal verbs to advise your reader, and imperative to add urgency?	
Have you grouped ideas and language in memorable ways, e.g. using a tricolon and alliteration?	
Does your conclusion urge your readers to take positive action?	

Assessing your writing

Assess your work based on these questions. Note any areas you need to improve.

Did the informality of your writing suit this genre? Did you address and persuade your audience?	
Which was your most convincing argument and why?	
Which was your most precise choice of words? What was your most emotive language?	
Can you improve the sequence of your arguments?	
Did a well-crafted conclusion leave your reader convinced?	

Writing a persuasive letter

This section builds on what you learnt about persuasive writing at Stage 7. Here, you will apply similar language techniques to the more formal genre of the letter. The reader of a letter is clearly identified, and may be an older person than you, in a position of authority. The language you use when writing a letter therefore needs to be formal and respectful. Persuasion needs to be gentle and, even better, supported by evidence.

A letter is intended to prompt a reply or response, so make it clear what you want your reader to do next. Think of the acronym **FLAP**:

> **F** = format: the kind of writing you are doing
>
> **L** = language features: the techniques needed to do the job
>
> **A** = audience: make sure your language suits your reader and his or her expectations
>
> **P** = purpose: keep this clearly in mind throughout and come back to it at the end.

There should not be more than five paragraphs in a formal letter. You are writing to a busy person and you need to get your ideas across concisely, without any unnecessary content. Paragraphs need to be short and purposive: make the topic quite clear throughout. Complex words and sentences will convey your authority and maturity.

Think of the acronym **CAPE**:

> **C** = clarity (it is clear what you want, why, and how your reader can help you)
>
> **A** = accuracy (the writing has controlled sentences and correct spelling)
>
> **P** = persuasion (you use language in a persuasive way)
>
> **E** = evaluation (you have considered both sides).

Over to you

Choose one task below. Use the checklists to plan, check and then assess your writing.

1. Write a letter to the leader of your local authority asking for better facilities for young people in your community.

2. Write a letter to a local newspaper arguing for improvements for cyclists where you live.

3. Write a letter to your school's governors suggesting ways in which your school could do more for the environment.

4. Write a letter to a local volunteer organisation of your choice to persuade the manager to let you join as a volunteer.

Planning your writing

Opening: state why are you writing to this person or organiation.	
Make your own views on the subject very clear and why you care.	
Support your views with facts and opinions, giving examples.	
Counter possible objections: evaluate and rebut them.	
End on a positive note: why would agreeing with you be better for everyone? What should be your reader's next steps?	

Checking your writing

Check your writing against this list. Improve your work as needed until you can tick each item.

Have you addressed your letter correctly? Have you greeted your reader formally and with appropriate language and politeness?	
Have you used the right modal verbs to make sure you convey your opinions strongly but not too forcefully?	
Have you used language as well as facts to show your expertise? Have you used longer words and sentences with authority and control?	
Have you made sure your paragraphs are linked by a topic sentence which also introduces the new subject?	
Do topic sentences make the subject of each paragraph clear and distinct?	
Have you used the features of persuasive writing?	
Have you used a variety of sentence types, and made sure longer sentences are punctuated correctly?	
Have you checked that your spelling follows the rules you have learnt? Have you included some of the more difficult words you have learnt?	
Is your letter the right length?	
Have you finished your letter by making a recommendation for action? Have you signed off correctly (have you checked the salutation and valediction)?	

Assessing your writing

Assess your work based on these questions. Note any areas you need to improve.

Was your letter both correct and interesting? Justify your answer.	
What should you aim to improve next time you do this exercise?	

Writing a persuasive speech

You have learnt that different kinds of persuasive or promotional writing have a lot in common. In all forms of persuasion, your audience comes first: you need to involve members of the audience and appeal to them in order to win their agreement. The format will decide whether your language is formal or informal. However, supporting facts and examples will always be important, as will an evaluation of counter-arguments and objections. There are lots of ways of using and organising language to make your writing more persuasive. Always keep the purpose of your task clearly in mind.

A speech will need to include informal language, close to the way we speak, although formality can come from the format (debates, for example, have rules and conventions). However, you also have a chance to add drama to your persuasion. You should vary the tone of your voice as well as your vocabulary. You can even use props.

Writing a speech is a tricky exercise. Some very good speakers don't use notes, or they go off their script. However, you need to be very confident to do this. It is best to begin by writing out speeches, then gradually move to using notes (cue cards) or memorising facts and details.

Your audience will be impressed by rhetorical or loaded questions and interesting ways of grouping words that make your speech memorable. However, you also need convincing facts to support your case, and real-life examples that will appeal to human interest.

Remember there is no right or wrong answer in a debate, only a more or less persuasive speech.

Over to you

Write a speech for or against any of these propositions.

1. Technology always improves the quality of our lives.
2. The advantages of genetically modified food are greater than the risks.
3. We should welcome living in a more international and globalised world.
4. The benefits of space travel are more important than its enormous cost.

Planning your writing

Opening: grab the audience's attention – tell a story or present some striking facts.	
Develop your argument with well-chosen examples, based on facts.	
Support your views with the opinions of others, especially experts.	
Evaluate counter-arguments and explain why the audience shouldn't worry about them.	
Speeches need a memorable conclusion, e.g. describe what the future will be like if everyone agrees with you.	

Checking your writing

Check your writing against this list. Improve your work as needed until you can tick each item.

Have you used informal language to get your audience's attention?	
Have you used technical language to show your know your facts?	
Do your sentences help you to vary the pace of your delivery: have you used short sentences for tension and urgency and longer sentences to show mastery of the topic? Check the transitional links.	
Are there quotations to support your views? Are there quotations to represent the opposition?	
Do rhetorical and persuasive features of language make your final paragraph memorable?	
Have you remembered to tell your audience which way they should vote?	

Assessing your writing

In the Checkpoint test, you will be assessed on content, structure, sentences and spelling, so these feature in the headings in this self-assessment grid.

Assess your work based on these questions. Note any areas you need to improve.

Content and purpose (8 marks) Was your material relevant and detailed?	
Structure and organisation (7 marks) Did you present your arguments in the right order and finish strongly?	
Sentences and punctuation (3 marks) Did you use long and short sentences accurately? Did they help the effectiveness of your writing?	
Spelling (3 marks) Did you spell technical words accurately? Are there any spelling rules you need to work on?	

Writing an informative summary

Writing an informative summary may not be the most exciting task, but it involves important skills. When writing a summary you are not only showing your understanding of a topic, but also communicating the most important information to your reader. You may be asked to research a topic and produce a summary to a word limit. It is important to keep within the word limit, to avoid repetition. Include as many details as you can. You need to select the most important details, and link and connect them.

In this kind of writing, facts are important. You need to sound neutral and unbiased. Leave out any opinions that are not supported by evidence. However, you are not presenting a set of bullet points or statistics: you will need to put information into your own words and to link your ideas. You are not allowed to use quotations or copy anything out from your original source material.

Along with formal letter writing, this is one of the most formal kinds of writing you will need to do. It therefore requires a strong stress on accuracy and good planning. To write a good summary, follow this six-step process.

1. Print and read your source material. Highlight the facts that are given – not the opinions.

2. Make a list of 15 key facts, putting these into your own words as you do so.

3. Work out the best way to reorder those facts, so that they suit your task and so that you can link the ones that are separate but related.

4. Now write out your summary in about 150 words, and about five sentences.

5. You must make sure you are using your own words throughout. Keep the tone formal (without abbreviations or contractions) but concise and detailed. Use the same tense as given in the task set or the source material (past or present).

6. Cut and re-draft your answer if it is longer than 150 words.

Over to you

Choose one of the following questions, to write your own informative summary, and select your own specific topic. Follow the six-step process above. Use an online or library reference book to find out the facts. Remember you need to present 15 pieces of information in 150 words (and five sentences). Do not include numbers, write in full sentences and link your ideas.

1. What makes a remote part of the world so different and interesting?

2. What are the most important things to see and do if you visit an important city on holiday?

3. Choose a scientific discovery. How did it take place and make a difference to our lives?

4. Describe the beliefs and traditions of people with a way of life very different from your own.

Planning your writing

Write each of your five sentences in one of the boxes.

Opening: make it relevant.	
Develop your point with supporting detail.	
Make a related point.	
Broaden out with further information.	
Link several facts that further support and develop your points.	

Checking your writing

Check your writing against this list. Improve your work as needed until you can tick each item.

Have you written no more than 150 words?	
Is your language precise and accurate?	
Have you presented 15 separate pieces of information?	
Is your language formal and without any abbreviations? Did you use the same tense as the question? Did you avoid personal opinions?	
Have you converted numbers and statistics into statements of fact?	
Is your writing neutral and objective?	

Assessing your writing

Assess your work based on these questions. Note any areas you need to improve.

Content and purpose (8 marks) What did you find most difficult about turning information into statements of fact for your summary?	
Structure and organisation (7 marks) What made linking and organising your sentences difficult? What might make this easier next time?	
Sentences and punctuation (3 marks) Did you keep your language consistently formal, and link and separate sentences correctly?	
Spelling (3 marks) Did you spell accurately? Did you find synonyms that helped you to use your own words? Did using a thesaurus help?	

Writing a mini-saga

Mini-sagas were invented as recently as 1982. A mini-saga is the literary equivalent of a 'tweet' (a 140-character message), but it tells a story with a beginning, middle and end, and does not just describe something. Writing mini-sagas has become a popular way of telling stories. Although very few words are used in a mini-saga, it is possible to create an atmosphere or situation, some development and some kind of ending or closure.

Writing a mini-saga will give you more practice in using language concisely and precisely. You need to use words with the maximum power and concentration, just as you would in a poem.

Over to you

Write a mini-saga consisting of *exactly* 50 words, not including the title. The title should have no more than 15 characters, but you can use it to explain the meaning of your story. Your mini-saga must tell a story with a beginning, middle and end. Leave out any unnecessary words and concentrate on the ones that describe a set of events. For this activity, abbreviations are allowed.

Planning your writing

Decide on a topic of your choice. Draft your ideas first, before reducing them to exactly 50 words, no more and no less! Use the grid below. If you need some help, you can use these three words:

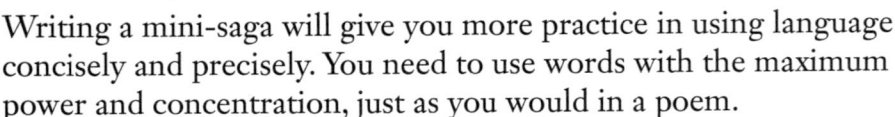

wretched   *exhilarating*   *radiance*

Opening: sketch out how you will introduce the topic and the atmosphere.	
Introduce an interesting development, conflict or change.	
Introduce another element.	
End the story: use a punchline for closure or finish with a cliff-hanger.	

Organise your story into 50 well-chosen words. Write each of your chosen words below.

Checking your writing

Check your writing against this list. Improve your work as needed until you can tick each item.

Does your story make sense?	
How are you going to arrange your paragraphs for maximum effect?	
Try your story out on a friend. Are there any improvements to make?	
Are there any words you want to change for something more atmospheric? (Use a thesaurus.)	
Does the ending of your story give your reader plenty to think about?	
Are all your sentences correctly punctuated and do they make sense?	

Assessing your writing

Assess your work based on these questions. Note any areas you need to improve.

Content and purpose (8 marks) What did you learn about stories by concentrating on telling a story in miniature?	
Structure and organisation (7 marks) What was most difficult about organising your paragraphs and different stages of your story? Did you manage to ensure that your story has a strong ending?	
Sentences and punctuation (3 marks) Does your punctuation clearly indicate where readers should pause and think about the meaning of your story?	
Spelling (3 marks) Extremely short pieces of writing need to be very accurate. How well did you balance interest and accuracy?	

Writing a myth of origin

Myths of origin tell us who we are and where we come from: they often involve the founding of a city or a tradition, or tell us how to treat one another. Myths of origin can also explain features of the natural world, including animals.

The hero (or heroine) is central to the myth. Usually, reluctant heroes are the best. They have a destiny, but rather than being boastful they are characters we can identify with. Other characters might include an amusing sidekick, a love interest, and a malicious enemy. What must the hero do to overcome his or her demons? What will be the consequences for the future?

Archaic features of language add to the power of myths, making myths sound as if they date from the time before we wrote things down. These features can be sound effects, such as alliteration or anaphora, or can help us to visualise characters and actions, such as similes, kennings or epithets. Longer, coordinated sentences can add to the epic quality of the writing.

Building paragraphs is especially important when you write a myth: you need to build towards a climax in your hero's adventure and then explain its importance. However, you need to begin with setting and character, and then explain the nature of the adventure your hero needs to go on.

The hero's choices must tell us something about how to behave, and the adventure should explain something about the real world.

Over to you

Choose one of the following scenarios to write a heroic narrative.

1. A conflict between two rivals leads to the founding of a mighty city.

2. An island arises from the ocean after a conflict between heroes.

3. A hero goes on a journey, gaining wisdom: at the end of the journey he or she is strong enough to face danger and save a city.

4. Your story and its hero explain how a tradition was first started.

Planning your writing

Opening: introduce the setting of your story and how your hero came to be involved.	
Develop your story by introducing a problem, a conflict or a task for your hero.	
Introduce examples of good and bad luck your hero encounters along the way.	
Write the climax: a conflict between your hero and a powerful enemy.	
In your conclusion, explain how the story has consequences even today. It is the origins of something we can now see in the real world.	

Checking your writing

Check your writing against this list. Improve your work as needed until you can tick each item.

Have you kept to the paragraph plan?	
Does your language suit a heroic and archaic setting? (You can use a dictionary or thesaurus to make your story sound more like a legend or myth.)	
Does your hero develop and learn from his or her experiences?	
Do these experiences form a model for us today?	
Is the enemy frightening and intimidating? Is this shown your dialogue?	
Does the ending celebrate and also explain the hero's story? Can you link it explicitly to the modern world?	

Assessing your writing

Assess your work based on these questions. Note any areas you need to improve.

Content and purpose (8 marks) Did your language and style match your purpose? Did you use language effects to add a heroic tone?	
Structure and organisation (7 marks) Did you manage the right balance for different stages of the story?	
Sentences and punctuation (3 marks) Did you vary longer and shorter sentences and punctuate dialogue accurately?	
Spelling (3 marks) Did you spell unusual words correctly?	

Writing a book review

A book review is both a record of what you have read and a recommendation to others. As usual, keep your audience in mind when writing in this genre. Use a friendly but fairly formal tone. If the book you are reviewing is fiction, take care not to give away any of the plot. Comments that do this are called spoilers: they spoil the story for other readers. This would go against your aim in writing the review, which is to make other people want to read the book.

Writers 'hook' their readers with exciting opening scenes and intriguing characters, and you can describe these in your review. Use quotations to give examples of what is good about the writing, followed by a short comment on why you think it is good.

Begin by introducing the genre of the book. What kind of book is it? What other kinds of book does it resemble? Show that you know the book's genre. What kind of reader would you recommend the book to, and why? What might potential readers of this book have already read that suggests they will like it?

Now introduce setting, characters and a little of the early action, through quotation. Leave description of the action on a cliff-hanger – if your readers want more they must read the book.

The best reviews comment on the style of the writer. Give an overall summary of what is best about the book, and perhaps a few suggestions about what might have been better.

Over to you

Choose a book you have recently read. Use the points above to structure a review of the book. You could present your review to your class, so that others find out about a book you have enjoyed.

Planning your writing

Opening: what made you choose the book? Say something about its genre and author.	
Introduce the setting and main characters. How do we get to know the characters and what kind of things do they say?	
Develop your ideas by choosing one or two key episodes from early in the story. Use quotations to illustrate them.	

Comment on the style in the quotations.	
State who should read this book and why.	

Checking your writing

Check your writing against this list. Improve your work as needed until you can tick each item.

Is your language precise and accurate? Have you used adverbs and/or adverbial phrases to describe the writing?	
Have you used and punctuated quotations correctly? Accuracy is essential!	
Have you remembered to follow quotations with some comment on the style the writer uses?	
Does your language convey your enthusiasm for the book and make your recommendation something the reader will pay attention to?	

Assessing your writing

Assess your work based on these questions. Note any areas you need to improve.

Content and purpose (8 marks) Did you keep your readers in mind throughout and structure the review based on what might interest them? Did you remember not to tell the story or reveal details of the plot? Did you keep up a friendly but fairly formal tone all the way through?	
Structure and organisation (7 marks) Did your writing have a clear introduction and conclusion? Did you use paragraphs and sequence your ideas, using sentences that formed links between paragraphs?	
Sentences and punctuation (3 marks) Did you vary your sentences for effect, using shorter sentences to express enthusiasm and longer ones to illustrate and explain?	
Spelling (3 marks) Did you spell words accurately? Did you find interesting longer words to describe what you found good about the book?	

Writing a features piece

Features writing is non-fiction writing that is not primarily about facts and information, but does not present opinions in a biased fashion either. This genre is used to write about difficult topics that don't have easy solutions. It allows you to present a topic in an intelligent and balanced way, looking at both sides of an issue, describing aspects in depth and making a careful evaluation. Instead of trying to demolish the opposition, in features writing you leave your readers to make their minds up for themselves.

This genre tests all your skills so far. You need to be able to separate facts and opinions and respect both. You also need to respect your readers, addressing them and informing them but not trying to impose your own bias.

To write a features piece for a newspaper or magazine, you need to think about how to put forward your own personal interest in the topic and how to introduce human interest by focusing on individuals and presenting their opinions through quotation. For higher marks you need to follow quotations with comments. You need to evaluate the strengths and weaknesses of what has been said.

Present your research in interesting ways. Start with a striking or unusual fact or opinion, or a personal anecdote. Use examples to illustrate your points. Use some of the ways you have learnt of grouping words and giving them rhythm. Involve your readers by using rhetorical techniques. Connectives are very useful in linking ideas, whether to provide further support for an argument or to highlight contrast.

An article for a newspaper or magazine does not need to be too formal – less formal than a letter, but more formal than a blog. You can use some of the language of speech, such as contractions, humour and a little slang. You need to keep the reader's interest.

In your conclusion, sum up what you have discovered. You might choose to give your own view here, but leave the final judgment to the readers. You should have given them enough material to make a decision.

Over to you

Choose from the following topics. Write an article of four or five paragraphs at most.

1. 'Behind the news' – write an article for a newspaper aimed at teenagers that explores the key arguments behind a topic in the news this week.

2. 'Education for tomorrow' – write an article for your school magazine on the skills students will need for the global workplace of the future.

3. 'Teenage tribes' – write an article for a music and fashion magazine on the music and trends fashionable among teenagers you know.

4. 'Making the world a better place' – write an article on what young people can do today to improve their environment and change attitudes.

Planning your writing

Opening: present the issues in a striking and interesting way, by telling a story.	
Develop your ideas with supporting facts and opinions.	
Give a contrasting example, which presents a very different viewpoint, and evaluate it.	
Explore what different people have said through quotation followed by comment.	
Address your readers directly and encourage them to make their own minds up by summarising the issues and asking the key questions.	

Checking your writing

Check your writing against this list. Improve your work as needed until you can tick each item.

Are your paragraphs sensibly structured and concise?	
Is your language lively enough to keep your audience interested?	
Have you used connectives to link your paragraphs?	
Have you punctuated quotations correctly?	
Did you avoid bias and give a balanced presentation to your readers?	

Assessing your writing

Assess your work based on these questions. Note any areas you need to improve.

Content and purpose (8 marks) Did you show that you had a sense of your audience?	
Structure and organisation (7 marks) Did you use paragraphing and links (cohesion) effectively?	
Sentences and punctuation (3 marks) Did you connect and divide sentences to best effect?	
Spelling (3 marks) Did you follow spelling rules, including for unusual vocabulary?	

Writing skills Stage 9

Responding to non-fiction or factual writing

As you approach the end of Checkpoint English, you will be assessed on your reading skills. This will consist of comprehension questions, which will test:

- knowledge of vocabulary and of language features (for example **simile** or **personification**)
- understanding of types of writing (for example travel writing, or advertising copy)
- your ability to analyse a writer's purpose and techniques.

Read the following text about a holiday destination and answer the questions that follow.

Your gate to paradise

Come and visit the island of Eleuthera, the sun-kissed crown jewel of the Bahamas.

Just imagine yourself away from the crowds on this unknown gem of an island. You'd think the beaches were there just for you. However, if that's not your thing, get yourself to Harbour Island and enjoy the casual sophistication of the five-star restaurants where you might easily find yourself sitting next to Hollywood stars at dinner.

It's not all beaches, swimming pools and sunloungers though. For those who want a more active holiday, scuba diving, kite surfing, snorkelling and sea fishing in the turquoise waters are all on offer.

Questions on language

1. Give two words which show that the island is a valuable treasure.

.... (2 marks)

2. Look at the expression *sun-kissed*. What is this expression an example of?

.... (1 mark)

3. What does *sun-kissed* suggest about the weather in Eleuthera?

.... (2 marks)

4. Look at this phrase: you might easily find yourself sitting next to Hollywood stars at dinner.

What does this suggest about Harbour Island? Underline one of the following sentences as your response.

   a It is a place inhabited by poor people.

   b Famous people go there for dinner.

   c The restaurants are very crowded.

   d The people of Eleuthera are very friendly.   (1 mark)

Questions on text type

5. What is the main purpose of this text?
   Give **two** details that support your answer.

   ....

   ....

   ....

   ....   (3 marks)

> **Advice**
> • Spend more time on responses that earn you more marks.
> • Only give the information requested. This is **not** a writing exercise.

Questions on purpose

6. In your own words, give three reasons why Eleuthera would be a good place to go for a family holiday.

   ....

   ....

   ....   (3 marks)

7. Choose three words or phrases from the passage. Complete this table, explaining briefly how the writer uses each one to persuade the reader that Eleuthera is an ideal holiday destination.

Word/Phrase	How this is used to persuade the reader

(3 marks)

Now check your answers!

Task, purpose and audience

Before you start producing writing of your own, you need to ask yourself three questions:

- What sort of text have I been asked to create?
- What are the rules or conventions of this genre of writing?
- Who will read this text?

For example, try to define four essentials for writing a formal letter. Think back to the acronym FLAP (on page 76.)

1. ....

2. ....

3. ....

4. ....

In your non-fiction writing you will probably be trying to do one (or more) of the following. Think about whether your aim is to:

- give information (for example in a news article)
- explain (for example in a recipe)
- argue or make a case (for example in a discussion)
- comment (for example in a report).

You need to be careful not to be condescending to (that is, to talk down to) the reader. You mustn't baffle the reader with specialist knowledge and long words either. Think about who is likely to read your writing and what the reader probably already knows.

> **Remember**
> Whatever genre of writing you are producing, the most important person to consider is your reader.

1. **Look at the list of text types at the top of page 93. Write the letter of each of these sentences against the correct text type in the list.**

   A Hi Ravi, just wanted to tell you I'm having a great time in Singapore. No probs with the flight. Hotel great.

   B In 1983, the American scientist and inventor, Thomas Edison, was experimenting with an incandescent electric filament light when…

   C Tommy, the blue tractor, was hungry.

   D Dear Mr Sanchez, Following our conversation yesterday, I am writing to you to agree that…

   E WYWH, CU 2moro

   F It is important to distinguish between the magnetic properties of iron and steel.

Text types:

- online encyclopaedia ....
- text message ....
- children's story book ....
- school text book ....
- letter from a bank manager ....
- informal email ....

2. **Either look at a text you have produced in the past or the extract about Eleuthera on page 90. Complete this table.**

Text type	
Purpose	
Audience	
Rules for this sort of text	1. 2. 3. 4.

3. Write a formal letter to a company in which you complain about something you have bought that has failed to live up to your expectations. In the letter explain why you feel that you have been misled by the advertisement you saw.

4. Evaluate your success in writing a formal letter by checking that you can answer 'yes' to these questions.

a Is the relationship between the reader and the writer clear throughout your letter?

b Is there a clear sense of the text type that was asked for? Check this against the four essentials you decided on earlier.

Choosing the right language and sentence structures

Language

Once you have thought about the text type and considered your potential readers, you need to decide what language will be appropriate.

As you have already seen (on page 26) it is important to think about the register of your writing (the level of language you use).

Remember

If you are writing in formal register, you should avoid slang, informal expressions or 'text-speak' unless you are using these features for a specific purpose.

1. **In your notebook, rewrite the following sentences more formally. Make sure you replace the underlined expressions.**

   a   He's <u>fed up</u> with his job and wants <u>to quit</u>.

   b   She's <u>been feeling out of sorts</u> since her grandmother got sick.

   c   He's got to <u>stop sitting on the fence</u> on this matter.

   d   She's a <u>pain in the neck</u> who doesn't know which <u>way is up</u>.

   e   My dad went <u>round the bend</u> when the car broke down.

   f   He <u>knocked off</u> and went home.

   g   She <u>burned her boats</u> when she failed to turn up to the interview.

   h   It's a <u>storm in a teacup</u>.

   i   My new computer cost me an <u>arm and a leg</u>.

   j   An opportunity like this comes along <u>once in a blue moon</u>.

2. **Look at the letter you wrote in answer to question 3, page 93. Pick out six words or expressions. Explain briefly why you thought they were suitable for the type of writing you were attempting.**

Word/Expression	Reason you chose it/Its effect

3. **Are there any words or expressions you would now change in your letter? List them in your notebook, and explain why you would change them.**

Sentence structure and effect

You have looked at several different sorts of sentence structure. It is important that, as with your choice of words, the shape of your sentence should suit the task. Look at this example:

> After the lettuce has been thoroughly washed in running water, it should be placed in a bowl.

It is easier to follow instructions if they are given as simple points:

> Wash the lettuce thoroughly in running water.

> Place the lettuce in a bowl.

It's often best to keep sentences short and simple. One reason for this is that you are more likely to make mistakes in grammar and punctuation when you write long sentences than when you write short ones.

Different types of sentence serve different purposes. Here's a rough guide.

Simple sentences:

- speed things up in a fast-paced narrative with lots of action
- emphasise a point
- make text easier to read than complex or compound sentences
- create atmosphere
- make good topic sentences in a paragraph.

Compound sentences:

- express more difficult concepts, linking ideas together in a complex way
- build up detail to create dramatic effect
- emphasise the importance of apparently insignificant detail
- lengthen time and action, possibly to heighten the drama of a scene
- can create a sense of innocence, for example as a young child writes, with everything equally important ('and then… and then').

Complex or complex compound sentences:

- are useful if your writing is very concerned with cause and effect.

Paragraph development

Every time you start a new paragraph, think about how you will structure it for maximum effect. Decide whether you are trying to:

- narrate (move chronologically through time)
- describe (give specific details about what something looks like, smells like or feels like)
- show process (describe step by step how something works)
- classify (explain one aspect of the topic you are discussing)
- illustrate (give examples to show your point).

You also need to think about how you create connections from sentence to sentence.

Look back to the work you did on connectives (on pages 6–7 and pages 31–32). Using as many connectives and phrasal connectives as you can, develop the following passage of nonsense in any way you choose.

Yesterday I went to the zoo to see the pink elephants. However, when I got there, it was shut. Consequently,

....

....

By the time I got there, ...

....

....

....

....

....

In your writing, remember to start a new paragraph when there is:

- a change of idea
- a change of focus.

As you write, think about the **purpose** of your writing. You might find it helpful to introduce supporting evidence to help you. That might consist of someone else's opinion or some facts.

At some point in the paragraph – it doesn't matter where – there must be a topic sentence. Everything else in the paragraph must be related to this central, controlling point.

> **Remember**
>
> When you work on structuring your writing, remember how useful connectives are for transition between paragraphs.

These are key elements that can be used when analysing paragraphs:

M main idea (topic sentence)

E evidence or facts

A analysis or comment

T transition to the next paragraph.

For example, if you are asked to write about the merits and interests of your home town, you might want to talk about its history, its facilities and its people.

Springfield is a great place to live. It has a long and interesting history dating back to the early 18th century. Its past can easily be revisited through a tour of the museum and the art gallery. It is famous for the generosity of its people (notably, they give more to charity per head than residents in any other small town in New Zealand). The fine schools, the sporting facilities, the theatre and the first-class hospital make Springfield an attractive place for both young and old alike. It is most famous, however, as the home of Uncle Bill's Rooftop Café.

You may never have heard of Uncle Bill's but....

Using a **MEAT** analysis, explain the function of each sentence in the extract.

1. ....

....

2. ....

....

3. ....

....

4. ....

....

5. ....

....

6. ....

....

7. ....

....

Creating an overall structure

You have been asked to write a short piece about how to repair a flat tyre on a bicycle. You decide on five paragraphs, each with one topic. Suggest a logical order for these topics, by writing the letters in your chosen order below.

A How to put the wheel back

B Encouragement to someone who is not confident that the task is quite easy

C How to remove the wheel

D Tips about what to do if things still don't seem right once the task is completed

E The equipment needed

....

The process of repairing a flat tyre requires tasks done in a logical order, and it's best to present the instructions in that order. Similarly, if you were asked to write about a day out, you would probably present things chronologically.

Getting ready to write

You have been asked to write an article entitled 'Five things to love about your friends'.

1. Write your plan for five paragraphs to cover the five things.

Paragraph 1: ....

....

Paragraph 2: ....

....

Paragraph 3: ....

....

Paragraph 4: ....

....

Paragraph 5: ....

....

2. Write your article in your notebook.

Look at question 3 below. In this case, you might want to produce a balanced essay – one that sees things from both sides. This question asks for an essay plan. Here are some points to help you.

- An essay plan should be only about 20–30 words: it is a plan, not a first draft.

- In your plan move away from a 'first this, then that' approach. Instead, link a series of paragraphs that argue a case.

3. **You have been asked to write an article for a school magazine in response to the question 'Should team sports be compulsory at my school?'.**

Plan a five-paragraph essay by filling in this table with your ideas. Include topic sentences.

	For	Against
Paragraph 1		
Paragraph 2		
Paragraph 3		
Paragraph 4		
Paragraph 5		

4. **Write the five paragraphs in your notebook.**

5. **Looking at your five paragraphs, check that you can answer 'yes' to these questions.**

- Is the material presented in a logical order?
- Is everything relevant to the topic I was given?

6. **If you are not using a sequencing or chronological principle, what is it that creates a logical sequence?**

....

....

7. **Write an article for a magazine entitled 'What should children do to help around the house?'.**

Beginnings and endings

Writing an opening paragraph

Once you have decided what you want to say, you need to introduce it. Often this is simply a matter of linking your paragraph ideas after you have written your text. If the whole piece makes an argument, you need to show how the ideas all link into a case that develops. You will probably want to write the introduction *after* you have written the bulk of the text.

Here is an opening paragraph from a student responding to the question you worked on earlier: 'Should team sports be compulsory at my school?'.

> Team sports inspire the healthy and talented to develop their skills. However, for many students whose skills and interests lie elsewhere, they are a nightmare. Rather than encouraging these students to take up activities that will keep them healthy in later life, the compulsion to join in puts them off all sorts of sporting activity. In the short term, these students live in dread of the next games session. In the long term, the students decide that sport of any kind is not for them and they give up on any activity that seems sports-related. The aim of school sport should be enjoyment for all in order to encourage a healthy lifestyle.

The writer uses connectives (see pages 7–8 and pages 31–32), introductory phrases and sub-clauses to allow the sentences to develop logically. These techniques make the reader aware that the writer is taking a comprehensive view and offering a balanced case.

1. Write the opening paragraph of your essay entitled 'Should team sports be compulsory at my school?'. Use your paragraph structure and topic sentences from page 99 as prompts.

Writing a conclusion

If you are writing to argue a case, you will need a conclusion.

Don't:

- say everything all over again
- introduce new material.

Do:

- explain how you have dealt with the task
- make your own view clear, if you have been asked to express it
- keep your conclusion short, particularly when writing in an examination.

2. Write the conclusion to your essay entitled 'Should team sports be compulsory in my school?'.

Evaluating your work

Look at the whole essay and ask yourself whether it contains the following elements or achieves the following goals. Give yourself a mark for the aspects listed.

Aspects	Mark
Relevant ideas and content are included, and developed with some detail Features of the text type are shown Suitable vocabulary is used	/8
A logical order is followed: introduction, main body, conclusion Paragraphs help to structure the text	/7
Appropriate sentence structures, designed for effect, help the text to develop Accurate grammar and punctuation are used	/7
Spelling is accurate throughout	/3

Learning from your experience

At the end of your essay, write a paragraph that summarises the strengths and weaknesses of your writing:

The strengths of this writing are:

....

....

....

The weaknesses of this writing are:

....

....

When writing like this in the future, I will need to:

....

....

....

Responding to fiction or descriptive text

The rules for responding to fiction in a comprehension exercise are very much the same as those for responding to non-fiction. This section gives an example then advice on answering different types of question.

Read the following passage.

Suddenly he emerged from the forest into an old road, and there before him saw, indistinctly, the figure of a man, motionless in the gloom. It was too late to retreat: the fugitive felt that at the first movement back toward the wood he would be ... "filled with buckshot". So the two stood there like trees, Brower nearly suffocated by the activity of his own heart.

A moment later – it may have been an hour – the moon sailed into a patch of unclouded sky and the hunted man saw that visible embodiment of Law lift an arm and point significantly toward and beyond him.

Ambrose Bierce

The easy marks in this sort of exercise come from identifying the **explicit**, surface meaning. Questions 1–4 are examples.

1. **Give two words that show that Brower has escaped from somewhere and is being chased.**

   .... (1 mark)

2. **Give a synonym for the word *embodiment*.**

   .... (1 mark)

3. **Explain in your own words the meaning of the word *significantly* as it is used in the extract.**

   ....

   .... (1 mark)

4. *So the two stood there like trees* **is an example of:**

   alliteration ☐

   hyperbole ☐

   metaphor ☐

   personification ☐   (1 mark)

Answering the more difficult questions in these exercises will require you to understand what is **implicit** in the text – the information you are not openly told but can work out. For example:

Question: How can you tell that Brower is frightened?   (3 marks)

Mark 1: Brower's heart is beating fast.

Mark 2: He seems incapable of movement.

Mark 3: It seems as though time has stood still.

5. What does: *So the two stood there like trees* show about the two men?

....

....

.... (3 marks)

Advice

- When answering this type of question, don't write more than is necessary.

- You won't be given bonus marks for giving additional information.

Advice

- When answering this type of question, you will need to make one statement for each of the marks.

The most complex questions will ask you to show understanding of the whole passage. Question 6 is an example. Notice that to answer this you have to say what is going on and then comment on its effect.

6. Explain in your own words how the writer uses contrasts and comparisons in these paragraphs to create tension.

....

....

....

....

....

....

....

.... (6 marks)

Advice

- To answer this type of question you have to analyse a whole passage, say what is going on and state what effect it has.

- As this is a more demanding task, the question is worth more marks.

Advice

- Allocate your time wisely, depending on the marks available for each question.

Writing fiction or description

Stages 7 and 8 covered writing different forms of fiction. The points in the checklist below are reminders of what you must do when you tell a story or write a description. Remembering this checklist will help you in the examination.

Checklist

Make sure that your material is relevant to the topic you have been given. ☐

Decide who is telling the story or doing the describing. ☐

Don't be too ambitious with plot (avoid using crashes, disasters, etc.). ☐

Think about the type of language you will use. ☐

Remember that you need to make the spelling, punctuation and grammar *correct* as well as effective. ☐

Decide on a balance between description (of character or place) and events. ☐

Think about the effect of different types of sentence (see page 95). ☐

Think about paragraphs and the effects gained by varying their length. ☐

Establish a clear time line for the story. ☐

Decide whether you want to include people talking. If you do, a new speaker should start a new paragraph. ☐

Remember that you will only be able to write a limited amount in the examination because you will only have around 30 minutes. ☐

Value quality over quantity. ☐

Check your writing for obvious mistakes. If you cannot spell a word, substitute one that you can spell. ☐

Possibilities for written tasks

1. **Choose one (or more) of these pieces to write your own story or description.**

   a Write a story in which someone makes an unexpected discovery about a friend or member of the family.

   b Write a story about two people who find themselves in a place they have never been to before.

   c Think back to when you were much younger than you are today. Describe a room in your house as you would have seen it then.

   d Describe a day out that you have had with friends or family.

   e Describe what you would do if you were headteacher of your school for the day.

Evaluating your work

2. Evaluate the strengths and weaknesses of the piece (or pieces) you have written. For each one, look at the whole piece and ask yourself whether it contains the following elements or achieves the following goals. Give yourself a mark for the aspects listed.

Aspects	Mark
Relevant ideas and content are included, and developed with some detail. Features of the text type (description or story) are shown. Suitable vocabulary is used.	/8
Ideas are developed, and there is an effective opening and ending. Paragraphs help to structure the text.	/7
Appropriate sentence structures help the text to develop and create effects, Accurate grammar and punctuation are used.	/7
Spelling is accurate throughout.	/3

Learning from your experience

3. Summarise the strengths and weaknesses of your writing, and list points to consider for future work.

The strengths of this writing are:

....

....

The weaknesses of this writing are:

....

....

When writing like this in the future, I will need to:

....

....

....

There are three main things that you can do to help you move onto the next stage.

- Develop your vocabulary.
- Read widely, attending to the rules and conventions of different genres of writing.
- Write in a variety of styles and forms, so that you can express yourself on paper in a number of different ways.

Develop your vocabulary

Using a dictionary

You may at some stage have wondered how useful a dictionary is if you cannot spell in the first place! As you move into the next stage of your course, you need to know how to use a dictionary to develop your vocabulary by looking up new and unfamiliar words and expressions when you come across them.

A dictionary tells you:

- how to spell
- how to pronounce words and phrases phonically (by sound)
- where a word comes from
- what part of speech a word is (and some words may belong to numerous categories)
- how a particular word is used in a variety of different ways, including in **idiomatic** expressions
- other words that are related to and derive from the one you are checking.

Look at this definition of the word *handle* from the *Concise Oxford English Dictionary* then answer the questions that follow.

handle • **v. 1** feel or manipulate with the hands. ➤(of a vehicle) respond or behave in a specified way when being driven: *the new model does not handle well.* **2** manage or cope with (a situation, person, or problem). ➤control or manage commercially. **3** deal with, ➤receive or deal in (stolen goods). **4** (**handle oneself**) conduct oneself. • **n. 1** the part by which a thing is held, carried, or controlled. **2** a means of understanding, controlling, or approaching a person or situation: *it'll give people some kind of handle on these issues.* **3** informal the name of a person or place: *that's some handle for a baby.* **4** the feel of goods, especially textiles, when handled. **5** US informal the total amount of money bet over a particular time or at a particular event.

– DERIVATIVES **handleability**/-'brlrti/ n. **handleable** adj. **-handled** adj. **handleless** adj. **handling** n.

– ORIGIN OE *handle* (n.), *handlian* (v.), from HAND.

1. What does *informal* mean in terms of word choice in writing?

   ....

2. You can use this word as both a .... and a ....

3. Use the expression *handle oneself* in a sentence.

   ....

4. Rewrite the following sentence without using the word *handle*. My new car does not handle well.

   ....

5. Write three sentences using the word *handle* as a verb in a different sense.

   ....

   ....

   ....

6. The cup had lost its handle could be rewritten with one of the derivatives of *handle*. Fill in the correct word: The cup was ....

7. What part of speech is the word that you have added to the previous sentence?

   ....

8. The man was arrested for handling stolen goods. What does this sentence mean?

   ....

9. Find out what *OE* means by looking in a dictionary list of abbreviations. If this abbreviation appears by a word in the dictionary, what does this tell you about the word's origins?

   ....

10. Write your own definition of the word *crash* and write five tasks (similar to the ones in the questions above) that you might give to a fellow student.

    crash: ....

    ....

    1. ....

    2. ....

    3. ....

    4. ....

    5. ....

    Once you have finished, check your definition in a dictionary.

11. Write out any elements of the definition that you missed.

    ....

Wider reading

Text analysis

The best preparation you can make for the next stage is to read widely. Precisely what you read isn't critical. What does matter, however, is that you read intelligently.

You should constantly think about a writer's techniques – about how a writer is saying something – as well as about what is being said. Filling in the table below will help you to analyse writing techniques in a structured way.

Look at an advertisement that tries to persuade you to buy something, then fill in this table.

Text title	
Text type	
Purpose	
Audience (age, gender, etc.).	
Rules for this sort of text	1. 2. 3. 4.
Language choice	
Structure	
Sentence structures	

You could do the same thing with every text you meet, even the back of a cereal packet!

In your reading you should include travel writing, advertisements, reference books, reports, leaflets, biographies, autobiographies, letters, diaries, journalism (in newspapers and magazines) and news websites.

Moving on

Now that you have analysed some text, you are in a position to deal with the most complex types of comprehension questions. Easy questions ask you to look at one aspect of a passage at a time. More difficult questions ask you to take a view of the whole passage and see how far its purpose is fulfilled. These questions also ask you to talk about the methods a writer uses, the *how* of the writing, rather than the content.

1. **Go back to page 90 and re-read the passage on Eleuthera. Fill in the gaps to answer the question: How does the writer make Eleuthera sound appealing to a variety of readers?**

   The title of the piece attracts because the metaphors of the **(a)** .... and of **(b)** .... in the title suggests that readers can enter into a new world. Adults might find the island appealing because the writer uses a metaphor such as **(c)** .... and the personification **(d)** .... to create a picture in the reader's mind. Children and teenagers would find the island appealing because the writer **(e)** .... in order to show the variety of activities that are available for younger holidaymakers. The writer's use of the words 'you' and 'yourself' has the effect of **(f)** ....

   The effect of dividing the information about Eleuthra into two paragraphs is that **(g)** .... and that **(h)** ....

Improving your writing

As you widen your reading, you will notice that some people write better than others. Some have more interesting ideas than others, or perhaps they express themselves better.

You can learn from other writers by imitating them and by trying to understand the form in which they are writing and the various choices they have made about language and structure. However, there are some principles of writing that are always sound, no matter what sort of text you are producing. Here are examples of what to avoid.

Features to avoid

Repetition

Avoid repetition, except for effect.

1. Read the following paragraph, then underline the repeated words.

> We found ourselves at a mysterious house. The air was full of mystery, and we were mystified and spooked by the door that seemed to lead nowhere. The mysterious noise we had heard coming from the house seemed to come from behind the door, and gave the house a spooky air. The mystery needed to be solved.

2. Write some other words that could replace the repeated words.

Repeated word	Replacement

Overworked words

It is best to widen your vocabulary. Varying the words you use will make your writing more interesting. For example:

He's a terrific dancer.

Here, *terrific* might be replaced with *talented*.

3. Write a more interesting word that might replace the underlined word in each of these sentences.

 a She's got a great new phone. ....

 b We had some nice apples yesterday. ....

 c Your new shirt is lovely. ....

 d She had an incredible time on holiday. ....

 e He wrote a fine short story. ....

Clichés (overused phrases)

Words or phrases that have been used repeatedly by speakers and writers are called clichés. They give a reader the impression that the writer is not thinking freshly about what needs to be said.

Clichés are often concealed **metaphors**. If you are not careful, literal meaning and the metaphorical can start to merge in an unintended way. For example:

The price of burgers, the company's bread and butter, had to increase.

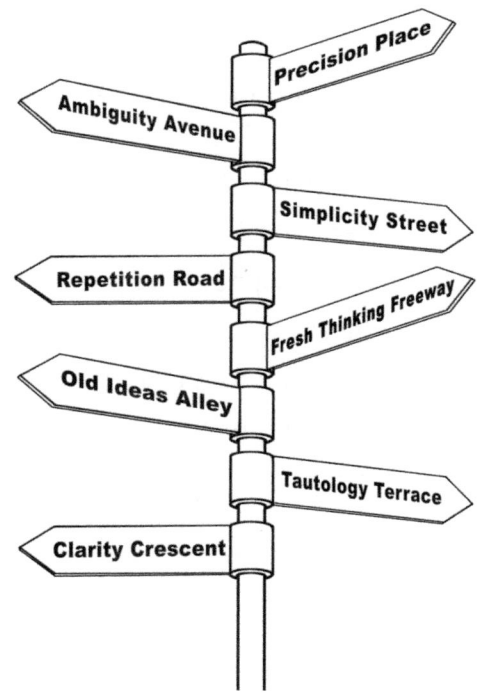

4. Rewrite the following sentences to avoid the clichés and metaphors.

a The clarinettist was as fit as a fiddle.

....

b My broken leg is a pain in the neck.

....

c We need to think outside the box about this problem.

....

Ambiguity

If a sentence is ambiguous, it means that it can be interpreted in different ways.

5. The following sentences are ambiguous because they are open to two interpretations. Rewrite each sentence so that it is no longer open to two two interpretations. Choose the interpretation that makes the most sense.

a If your eye falls on a bargain, pick it up.

....

....

b If the baby won't eat the food, throw it away.

....

....

c He gave her cat food.

....

....

d The girl looked at the boy with the telescope.

....

....

Tautology

Tautology is repetitive use of words or phrases that have the same meaning.

1. **In each sentence below, underline the word or phrase that results in the same thing being said twice.**

   a The annual New Year's Eve party takes place every year on 31 December.

   b I went to the shops personally.

   c We need a new hot water heater.

   d The storm hit at 1 a.m. in the morning.

   e In my opinion, I think he is wrong.

   f Lara completed the assignment by working through the points in her essay plan one after the other in succession.

Verbosity

Verbosity is using many words when one or two will serve your purpose and make your writing easier to understand. Try to say things concisely, using uncomplicated language. Remember that, unless you are aiming for a particular effect, short sentences are clearer and easier to read than long ones.

Compare the following two sentences.

Food intake predicts body mass index according to a monotonically increasing relation.

If you eat more, you will put on weight.

It's obvious which sentence is clearer and easier to read. You should aim for the same clarity in your own writing.

2. **Rewrite the following sentences to convey the same meaning without the excess words.**

   a At this moment in time, the company's production facilities confront ongoing labour-related challenges that impact on successful realisation of innovative product delivery in the market place.

   ....

   ....

   b Participants were tested under conditions of good to excellent acoustic isolation.

   ....

   c In view of the fact that play has been suspended for the duration of the inclement weather, the question as to whether it will re-start remains unresolved.

   ....

   ....

3. Strike through any words in the following passage that could be missed out with no change to the sense. You will need to insert the word *by* at two points.

> The organisers of the public display should try to achieve greater safety both from the point of view of ensuring that the bonfire itself does not contain any unacceptably dangerous materials such as discarded aerosol cans or foam furniture and from the point of view of ensuring the letting-off of fireworks in the designated area only, with easily identifiable wardens to be available during the event to prevent people indiscriminately letting off fireworks, to the possible danger of people attending the event.

4. To make it still easier for a reader to understand, make the extract into two sentences.

....

....

....

....

Passive writing

Writing in the passive voice (see page 16) has its place, particularly in scientific writing, where the agent (the person doing the action) is less important than the action itself. For example:

> The chemical was placed in a test tube before being heated.

It is not important *who* did the placing.

However, you should try to avoid passive constructions because they make writing less vivid.

Passive (to be avoided): The rabbit was bitten by the cat. Active (preferred): The cat bit the rabbit.

         Five cakes were baked by my mother.   My mother baked five cakes.

The passive can, of course, be used for a change of emphasis, perhaps to make things less aggressive. Supervise your children at all times (active) is much more bossy than Children must be supervised at all times, (passive).

To sum up

When you write, you should try to obey some simple rules

- Be polite to your reader — give as much information as is needed to get your point across and no more
- Ensure that what you write is relevant to the given task
- Avoid lazy writing that uses tired, over-used expressions
- Be brief, clear and logical in what you are saying, unless you are trying for a specific effect which involves breaking this rule
- Avoid obscurity and possible misinterpretation: choose simple words over difficult words where possible.
- Above all, always write with specific readers in mind. Aim to please them.

> Decide whether to use the active or passive voice by thinking about the impression you want your writing to give.
>
> For example, use the active voice for informality, immediacy and urgency; use the passive for formality, neutrality (for example when writing about a scientific experiment) or perhaps to create a sense of mystery.

Answers

Chapter 1
Page 4

1. **a** was
   b was born
   c are performed
   d were borrowed
   e make

2. Anjali and Paul approached the old farmhouse cautiously. They knew it was meant to be empty. They opened the cobweb-covered barn door. Something dark flew out straight towards them. They recovered slowly from the shock. A man was standing in front of them. He was staring straight at them.

Page 5

1. **a** quickly
   b happily
   c simply

2. **a** steadily
   b accidentally
   c terribly
   d narrowly
   e fully

3. I am writing to apologise fully for the mistake I made. I came into the classroom noisily to fetch my bag. I did not realise the class inside were silently working on a test. I behaved selfishly and irresponsibly.

Page 6

1. **a** The sun was shining <u>and</u> every one looked forward to a good day.
   b They were all ready for the beach <u>but</u> they had to find the quickest way to get there.
   c The fast train left later <u>or</u> they could take the slower bus.

2. **a** or
   b and
   c but
   d but
   e and

3. **a** The players played bravely to the end <u>but</u> they were defeated <u>and</u> the crowd did not forgive them.
   b Shiv needed help with his homework <u>or</u> he could borrow someone else's <u>but</u> he knew he would not learn anything that way.
   c Tracey wasn't good at computer games <u>but</u> she could ask her brother to help her <u>or</u> she would take forever to move to the next level.

4. You can easily see the connection between the different statements.

Page 7

1. **a** preposition (into)
   b conjunction (as)
   c both (since)

2. **a** through (preposition)
   b Although (conjunction)
   c until/before (preposition)
   d beside (preposition)
   e in order to (conjunction)

3. **a** you and me
   b beyond
   c from
   d from
   e to
   f of
   g among
   h in
   i with
   j to

Page 8

1. **a** because
   b Although
   c which

2. **a** Although
   b who
   c until
   d whilst
   e because… despite

3. You can rearrange the notes in different ways. These are the conjunctions or relative pronouns to use: although, since, therefore, which, 'despite' at the beginning of the sentence, or 'but' in the middle.

Pages 9–10

1. **a** Although food is essential for our good health, we need to be careful what we eat.
   b We need a balanced diet, which consists of carbohydrate, proteins and unsaturated fats.
   c While the main food types are all essential, they do need to be kept in the right balance, as an excess of any one type can lead to health problems.

2. **a** While/As
   b because
   c unless/even though/until
   d Even though
   e Although
   f As… wherever
   g whereas
   h Whenever

3. **a** I saw a woman wearing a large hat as/while I was walking down the street.
   b Because he had prepared for it thoroughly, Karl passed the test.
   c Unless/Even though she had plenty of wet weather clothing, she did not want to go to Wales again!

d She had got used to hearing the music every day even though she never liked it.

e I did not want to go on although I did not want to turn back.

f Wherever you looked, there were golden leaves brightening the gaps between the trees as you walked through the autumn woods.

g For Sunita the task was much more difficult whereas Ali found it easy.

h I felt I had stepped into a different and happier world whenever I crossed the narrow strait to the island.

Page 11

1. **a** object (third person singular) – him
b possession (third person singular) – his
c subject (first person plural) – we
d object (third person plural) – them

2. **a** they
b me
c you
d he
e their

3. Rick is making good progress in English. *His* comprehension skills… . *He* can write good stories. … I have given *him* extra exercises to help him with this. *His* class also visited the theatre where they enjoyed the play… . *Their* reviews of the performance were lively and *his* was the best of all.

Page 12

1. **a** her
b their
c were

2. **a** was
b ran
c are
d want
e has

3. Travelling to unusual countries *gives* you… different people *tell* you… . Wandering off the tourist trail *lets* you… . The sights and sounds *are* unusual… Try anything once, is what I always *say*… many believe different types of tea *have*… and the experience *is*… Strong spices *have*… many meals which *were* cooked to perfection. Most cultures… *bring* you….

Page 13

1. **a** best
b louder
c bravest

2. **a** that
b which
c who
d whom
e whose

3. comparative: "faster and more urgently"
adjectival clause: ("which was" is understood and left out) "advancing with terrifying speed"
compound adjective: "foamy-white"
superlative: "scariest"
adjectival clause: "which gave him hope".

Page 14

1. time – as soon as
manner – how
place – where
reason – since
result – so that
condition – if
concession – although

2. **a** When
b in order to
c since/because/as
d despite

3. *Treasure Island* was written by Robert Louis Stevenson <u>in order to give</u> children the thrill of adult adventure. He chose Jack, a boy narrator <u>so that</u> you feel Jack's terror and his growing confidence. <u>Although</u>, he doesn't get much help from other adults, he finds a way to outwit the pirates <u>as</u> they fight among themselves. He thinks quickly and decisively <u>about whether</u> he can exploit this situation.

Page 15

1. **a** met
b shone
c told

2. **a** dug
b held
c stuck
d brought

3. We <u>kept</u> the fishing rods in the shed and <u>brought</u> them out when we <u>had</u> a spare weekend. Many fish <u>swam</u> along this stretch of the river. We <u>cast</u> out our lines. The rods <u>bent</u> as the fish <u>bit</u> the bait. When we <u>caught</u> them, we <u>slid</u> them off the hook and <u>placed</u> them back in the river. We <u>left</u> when the sun <u>went</u> down.

Pages 16–17

1. **a** Passive
b Active
c Passive

2. **a** were given
b played
c grazed/were grazing
d was broken
e gave

3. **a** News of his university place was received by Carl this morning,
b The lawn was mowed by his father every Sunday.
c The door had been forced open by burglars.
d A satisfactory reason for the team's performance was not given by the manager.
e As the silver nitrate was added, a white precipitate was observed by the laboratory technician.

Pages 17–18

1. **a** adverbial
b adverbial
c adjectival

2. *Sample answers:*
a bravely and forcefully
b completely and utterly
c foolishly and irresponsibly
d extremely fluently
e quite abruptly

3. *Example answers:*
a swiftly and safely
b eerily profound
c darkly and ominously
d quickly and cheerfully
e roaring and crackling
f energetically and enthusiastically
g funny, creepy and amusing
h very inspired
i imaginatively and interestingly
j fascinating and unusual

Pages 18–19

1. **a** will
b should
c might

2. **a** Can
b may (or could)
c might
d should
e ought
f might
g could
h should
i can
j would

3. **a** could
b might
c shall
d should
e may

Page 20

1. prefixes: (a) un–, (b) in–; suffix: (c) –able
2. **a** il– (illiterate)
b ir– (irreparable)
c im– (immortal)
d mis– (misspelt)
e un– (unnatural)
3. **a** outrage<u>ously</u> <u>under</u>represented
b <u>sub</u>conscious intui<u>tion</u> danger<u>ous</u>
c <u>super</u>numerary impress<u>ive</u>
d disappear<u>ance</u> <u>extra</u>ordinary
e disgrace<u>ful</u> coward<u>ice</u> <u>dis</u>trusted

Page 21

1. **a** synonym
b antonym
c synonym

2. **a** bold
b deceive
c tune
d hunt
e condolence

3. **a** unhappy
b talk up
c taught
d emotional
e ordinary
f happy
g miserable
h unobtrusive
i humble
j too little

Page 22

1. **a** across
b to
c before
2. **a** behind that hill and across the valley
b On the other side of the narrow bridge over the highway
c Under such circumstances
d through the rain-soaked marshes
e over the steep incline of the mountainous region
3. **a** Beneath/Under
b before
c across
d Before

Pages 23–24

1. **a** In the cool shade of the woodland
b tentatively
c an instinctively cautious boy,
2. **a** Quickly but confident that he knew what he was looking for, my business-like father zapped his way through the various channels.
b Dully-dressed experts, marching across old battlefields, explained the history behind them, animatedly waving their arms in the air.
c Briskly marching across the living room, my mother, seizing the controller, asked "Can't we watch something else?"
d Suddenly, the screen was filled with vacuous celebrities, exchanging gossip about movie stars.
e I said I was going upstairs, where my glowing laptop, full of messages and pictures from my friends, was waiting for me.
3. By forcing defeated nations to the conference, the victorious powers ensured peace treaties were signed, despite their humiliating terms of surrender.
4. The emphasis is now on the humiliation of the defeated nations rather than the vigorous actions of the victorious powers to ensure peace. This sentence sees the treaties more from the point of view of the defeated nations. The bias has shifted slightly but significantly.

Page 25

1. **a** wrong
   b correct
   c correct
2. **a** I always find writing stories difficult. I tend to leave them to the last minute.
   b Ben preferred to have a light on when he went to bed. He was afraid of the dark.
   c He woke up to find his body distending and his arms and legs shrunken. He had become a giant beetle.
   d As the Lilliputians thought about the huge size of the giant, they realized how they could make him useful. He could help them win their war against the Blefuscans, their old enemies.
   e Digging further beneath the surface, they discovered the traces of a much older city. There were ancient bricks and curious fragments of pottery and metal.
3. A semi-colon – using a semi-colon makes the connection between what is in the two different parts of the sentence very clear. The effect of the punctuation is to have less drama and more logic. Think about this when writing arguments, rather than narratives.

Pages 25–26

1. **a** A speech to your classmates **2**
   b A letter to a friend. **3**
   c A report to a committee of teachers and other adults **1**
2. **a** formal
   b informal
   c informal
   d formal
   e informal
3. **a** informal
   b informal
   c formal
   d formal
   e informal
   f informal
   g formal
   h formal
   i formal
   j formal

Page 27

1. **a** In two years' time it's going to be a leap year.
   b It should've been Lohit's turn next.
   c I didn't think you'd call me.
2. **a** Who's
   b Whose
   c There's
   d Their
   e You're
3. **a** They've… cats'…
   b Don't… you've… You're…
   c Let's… they're… our…
   d could've… weren't…
   e I'm… it's…

Page 28

1. **a** her
   b yours
   c theirs
2. **a** whom
   b whose
   c Those
   d that
   e This
3. Which – **questioning** to involve those listening you… yourselves – **reflexive** to emphasise women's rights
   those – **demonstrative** to stress those who are silent
   who – **relative** to show they are many but are not allowed to be individuals or be named.

Page 29

1. **a** them;   **b** you;   **c** my
2. **a** Bo told us to say that the work had been done by <u>you and me</u>.
   b Whenever I tried to tell them off, <u>they</u> wouldn't listen to me
   c We wanted to play outside but it rained all day so <u>our</u> games had to be indoor ones.
   d Between you and me, <u>they</u> don't have any chance of winning it.
   e I'm not going to tell you what to do, that's for <u>you</u> to decide.
3. Juan and Angela were playing outside. Their father Adolfo was indoors reading a book. He put it down and asked <u>them</u> if <u>they</u> would like some sandwiches. <u>They</u> said that was just what <u>they</u> needed, so he made some sandwiches. When he came back, <u>Juan</u> and Angela were using badminton rackets. When they finished, they packed them up and he gave them <u>the sandwiches</u>.

Page 30

1. **a** dry-cleaning
   b bedroom
   c swimming pool
2. **a** affected
   b compliment
   c allusions
   d illicit
3. **a** explicit
   b inhumane
   c disinterested
   d principle

Page 31

1. **a** nevertheless: contrast
   b therefore: conclude
   c additionally: develop
2. **a** moreover
   b consequently
   c equally
   d Finally
3. **a** no
   b yes
   c yes
   d no
   e yes

Page 32

1. **a** even though – concession
   b all things considered – reason/purpose
   c exclusive of – exception
2. **a** Despite
   b To this end
   c Granted that
   d with the exception of
   e That being the case
3. Students' own answers.

Pages 33–34

1. **a** The football players were talking to the fans, who were overawed.
   b The old man, who was smoking a pipe, sat next to the boy.
   c The police questioned the youths, who were very embarrassed, about the incidents the previous evening.
2. **a** In this country tigers can be seen in their natural habit.
   b Sunrise is the best time to see animals gathering around the waterhole
   c Wilderness was all around them as they waited for rescue.
3. 1 A simple sentence is used to catch the reader's attention.
   2 The first person plural pronoun involves the reader.
   3 A rhetorical question and second person pronoun engage the reader's thoughts and feelings.
   4 A complex sentence appears, including a list and a prepositional phrase.
   5 A short, simple and colloquial sentence also involves the reader.
   6 Inversion is used in order to give a sense of place.
   7 A parenthetical phrase appears, for additional explanation.
   8 The second person pronoun addresses the reader directly.
   9 Inversion is used for emphasis (note use of pronouns).
   10 A connective is used for contrast, twice, in a sentence with complex and compound elements.

Page 35

1. **a** parallelism
   b tricolon
   c inversion
   d alliteration

2. **a** tricolon
   b parallelism
   c inversion
   d alliteration
   e tricolon/repetition

3. We were ~~totally and utterly unanimous~~ unanimous in agreeing that this was outrageous. We had seen it ~~with our own eyes~~ and knew her self-defence ~~of herself~~ was ~~over~~ exaggerated and her excuse not sufficient ~~enough~~ to justify what she did.

Chapter 2
Page 36

1. **a** I've never heard of pink elephants loose on the road before.
   b I want to buy apples and pears when I go shopping in the market!
   c Noor flew to New York and Paris last year.
   d Crying won't help you – it's broken.
   e 'Pirates of the Caribbean' is my favourite film.

Page 37

2. **a** We went to Argentina for our holiday. I wanted to sample the food. My mother and sister wanted to learn the tango. My brother was keen to see the football.
   b My father works in Bangalore. He is 40 years old. My mother is 38. They both have full-time jobs.
   c The school magazine has just been printed. It is available from the office. It can be sent out by post if requested. Many of the students have contributed articles or artwork.
   d I like to watch television in the evening. My favourite programmes are soap operas. I never watch the news. I never watch during the day. I have too much to do.

Pages 38–39

1. Victoria Falls was first seen by Europeans in 1855. It is 1708 metres wide and 108 metres high. It is the largest sheet of falling water in the world. It is on the Zambezi river. Victoria Falls is also called by its original name Mosi-oa-Tunya. The falls is at the border between Zambia and Zimbabwe. It is now a popular tourist destination. About a million tourists visit each year. The falls can easily reached by bus and train. The area round the falls is popular for adventure sports.
2. Victoria Falls, on the Zambezi river, is 1706 metres wide and 108 metres high and is the largest sheet of falling water in the world. On the border between Zimbabwe and Zambia, Victoria Falls is also known by its original name Mosi-oa-Tunya. First seen by Europeans in 1855, it is now a popular tourist destination with around a million visitors each year.

The area round the falls is popular for adventure holidays and can easily be reached by bus and train.

Pages 39–40

1.

Hi Hanna,
Wow! That was my first thought on seeing Mosi-oa-Tunya. What a waterfall! That was my immediate reaction to the highlight of my holiday in Africa. Am I really here? Amazing! All that water. All that noise. Who would have thought I would ever have seen such a glorious sight? It was one of the most memorable moments of my life. Enough. Hope all well with you. Must rush.

Rachel

2. a The person was asked whether he or she had any qualifications to teach English.
  b They were asked if they all understood how that program worked.
  c Sharon was asked when Steve would arrive.
  d The question was what would happen to them next.
  e They questioned whether they could be sure that this was the right answer.
3. The concert was just incredible. We heard all our favourite band's greatest hits. The performance just blew your mind away! Can you imagine what it is like to be surrounding by hundreds of screaming fans? I was asked to their next gig too.

Pages 41–42

1. a He always takes pens, compasses, pencils, rulers and correction fluid into exams.
  b She thinks he is stupid, dull and unimaginative.
  c The boy reached the gate, hopped over, and continued down the path.
  d Although it was not expensive, the dress looked fabulous.
2. a Indeed, only when we see the results will we know whether the students have passed, failed or gained scholarships.
  b Her writing was described as interesting, lively and stylish.
  c Any decent kitchen will have sharp knives, wooden spoons, plastic mixing bowls and lots of metal pans for the oven.
3. As you probably already know, in order to be fully fit you need to eat a balanced diet. Sweets, chocolates, crisps, sugary drinks and cake, though providing variety, do not give you the vitamins, minerals and dietary fibre that are essential to a busy healthy lifestyle. It is, of course, perfectly possible to live your life without eating meat. Indeed, many people think that a fully vegetarian diet that contains beans, pulses and cereals as well as a wide variety of the more obvious vegetables — carrots, potatoes, cabbage, tomatoes, etc. — is the best option. Whatever you choose to eat —whether you are vegetarian, vegan or meat eating — the most important thing seems to be that you should eat in moderation and ensure that you consume nutritious, tasty food from a wide variety of food groups each day.

4. Although I like hot weather, I don't like to lie out in the sun. My brother does. When we were on holiday last summer, he spent too much time by the pool. This meant that I didn't get the opportunity to see all the monuments, museums and art galleries. It was a shame, as I had hoped to improve my knowledge of Indian culture and history. I met some interesting people from all over the world, of course. However, on the whole, the holiday was a bit disappointing.

Page 43

1. a If you are going to India, you ought to see the Taj Mahal, The Red Fort, and New Delhi.
  b It is easy to use a smart phone: even my grandma knows how to text.
  c Please bring at least one of the things from the following list: a tent, a change of clothes and enough food to last 24 hours.
  d She did very well in the national competition: she won second prize.
  e I went shopping and bought a kettle, a saucepan and a knife.

Pages 44–45

1. [because]… the first part of the sentence promises an example which the second part then delivers.
2. a He loves maths; she can't stand it.
  b Our school specialises in music and the arts; the one down the road is more focused on sports.
  c We wanted to eat hamburgers and chips; my mother had different ideas.
  d The winters in Canada are cold and long; in Florida, however, they hardly even exist.
3. Students' own answer.
4. He saw the shape of a giant towering above him: it was Grendel's mother. She pinned him down; she pulled a knife. This looked like the end: Beowulf feared that it was. However, the knife was blunt; Beowulf's armour was strong. He seized the sword; with one stroke he swung round; instantly, the monster was dead. He had displayed the courage of a true hero: superhuman effort; determination stronger than that of lesser men; fearlessness in the face of almost certain death.

Answers

Page 46

1. The half-deaf lady was ninety-four years old. Her good-for-nothing grandson never visited, except to take her to the end-of-term party. She usually arrived with home-made jam in mis-labelled jars. Without fail, the lady and her grandson were precisely twenty-five minutes late.

2. a A walking-stick is very useful in the hills.
   b "There is a man-eating tiger outside," she cried.
   c Extra-curricular activities are really important at our school.
   d He gets three-monthly bank statements.
   e The one-armed man guarded the bank vault.

3. Students' own answers.

Page 47

1. a The whole holiday – the tickets, the airport, the hotel, the food – was a disaster.
   b There is something I need to tell you – it won't be a surprise.
   c We watched a film – quite entertaining if I remember rightly – on the first night of the holiday.
   d Intelligence, good humour, sporting ability – all of these are typical of my sister's friends.

2. a Please ask the secretary (room 64) if you need an application form.
   b You need to add two tablespoons (40 grams) of honey.
   c There is more on this in Chapter 4 (pages 19–20).
   d London (in Ontario) is home to a number of universities.
   e We had bought tickets to the show in advance (they were very hard to get) rather than just turning up on the night.

Page 48

1. Sentence a is incorrect because the sentence is two separate sentences wrongly joined by a comma (a comma splice).
   Sentence f is incorrect because two separate sentences are linked with an attempt to cover this link by using a comma and *however*.

2. b This sentence contains two equally important things to remember.
   c This one gives something important to remember and a piece of supplementary information.
   d Here there is something important to remember and a warning or reminder about the briefing.
   e This is like sentence b, but the *however* makes the second clause a stronger reminder.

Pages 49–50

1. a The children's toys were lying all over the floor.
   b Rakesh's clothes were all in a pile near the door.
   c The teachers' day room was always packed at recess.
   d The table's legs were wobbly.
   e In two weeks' time, my holiday starts.
   f In one month's time, my sister is expecting a baby.

2. a the girl's friend's bag
   Girls = 1   Friends = 1
   b the girls' friends' bag
   Girls = 2 or more   Friends = 2 or more
   c the girl's friends' bag
   Girls = 1   Friends = 2 or more
   d the girls' friend's bag
   Girls = 2 or more   Friends = 1

Pages 50–51

1. I won't be able to come to the party. I can't even get out of bed just now because I'm ill. I haven't been out for some days. You can tell me what's been happening at school. I'd bet that no one's doing any work because it'll soon be the holidays. I can't imagine that I'll be back before the break. You'd better give my best wishes to everyone. Don't forget that you're invited to my birthday party next month.

2. a I'm going to cook carrots this evening.
   b There's nothing that you can do about the situation. He will never change his mind.
   c The women's shoes are over there.
   d He'll never go there again – it's a terrible place.
   e I can't hear you.
   f Priya's homework is always perfect.
   g I couldn't come because I've been busy.
   h Who's coming to town with me?
   i Whose coat is this?
   j We'd love to come to the party.

Page 53

1. a Is 'curiouser' really a proper word?
   b 'I'll be back' is a famous line from the film 'The Terminator'.
   c He always watches the programme 'Africa' on Thursdays.
   d She wanted to know if he had visited the Chhatrapati Shivaji railway terminus in Mumbai on his journey, as it was used as a setting in 'Slumdog Millionaire'.
   e I can't remember which of Shakespeare's plays includes the speech 'To be or not to be'.
   f Did you go to the Boston Red Sox game yesterday?

Page 54

"Tell us a story!" said the March Hare.

"Yes please do!" pleaded Alice.

"And be quick about it," added the Hatter, "or you'll be asleep before it's done."

"Once upon a time there were three little sisters," the Dormouse began in a great hurry, "and their names were Elsie, Lacie and Tillie, and they lived in the bottom of a well."

"What did they live on?" said Alice who always took a great interest in questions of eating and drinking.

"They lived on treacle," said the Dormouse after thinking a minute or two.

"They couldn't have done that you know,' Alice gently remarked. "They'd have been ill."

"So they were," said the Dormouse, "*very* ill."

Page 56

1. **a** said
   b had cheated
   c must be made/had been made

2. **a** Seun said that he would make sure he had the right books with him next time.
   b Pam insisted that John should keep away from the edge of the platform.
   c Paul claimed that it was Mary's turn to do the chores that day.
   d The man at the warehouse promised that they would deliver the goods on time.
   e The prisoner in the dock shouted out that he had not done it.

3. "I'll make sure everyone has early notice of the date for the fundraising party," said Amar.
   "The date needs to be fixed quickly so that we can advertise on the website," said Jules.
   "I still need to confirm the availability of the hall," explained Amar.

Page 57

He asked if she had seen the first episode of 'My Brilliant Friend' last night. She replied that she had not seen it. Her parents wanted her to go and see an awful kids' film called 'Fishy' instead. He replied that he did not much like children's films these days, though he had enjoyed 'Islands of Adventure', and that he really liked the song 'Sing it Loud'. She said she thought he was joking because she had thought of him as more of a suspense film fan.

Pages 57–58

1. **a** prove
   b practise
   c seasonable
   d precedes
   e respective
   f aisle
   g creek
   h heard… herd
   i hangers
   j muscles
   k flair
   l dual

2. I have a spelling checker
   It came with my pc
   It plainly marks for my review
   Mistakes I cannot see.
   I strike a key and type a word
   And wait for it to say
   Whether I am wrong or right
   It shows me straight away.
   As soon as a mistake is made
   It knows before too long
   And I can put the error right
   It's rarely ever wrong.
   I have run this poem through it
   I am sure you're pleased to know
   It's letter perfect all the way
   My checker told me so.

   —Source unknown

Page 58

1. **a** Jasbir and I went out to town on Saturday.
   b Correct
   c There were many <u>fewer</u> people there by the end of the day than there had been at the beginning.
   d Correct
   e You need to make <u>fewer</u> mistakes with your homework.
   f Between you and <u>me</u>, she needs to improve her work if she wants to go to college.
   g I didn't do <u>anything</u> to break the window.
   h We're ~~like~~ just waiting to go away. We really like visiting the countryside.

Page 61

My First Car

1. For years I have been driving an old, used car with a lot of mileage. I hate it. It gets me where I need to go, but I'm tired of fixing its leaks and broken parts all the time. It annoys me every time I need to take it to the mechanics at the garage. Even when they take care of everything, I know I'll just end up going back shortly with some new problem.

2. Finally, I have decided that, even though I can't afford it, I need to buy a new car. Unfortunately, I have a problem: I have no idea what car to get. Do I want something big? Do I want something fast? Something economical? I have so many choices that I don't even know where to begin.

3. I'm not sure if I will be able to make a decision on my own. As I said, I don't have a lot of money either, so I will probably have fewer options. After I did some research, I decided I would need some expert advice.

4. On Friday I went to a local dealership to check out some new models. I talked to the salesperson, and listened carefully. Her honesty and professionalism were really impressive. She had a lot of very helpful suggestions and she showed me some current models from a limited number of affordable choices. After a long discussion, I finally decided which one I wanted.

Chapters 3–4

Students' own answers.

Chapter 5

Many of the answers in this chapter will be students' own. Where we can, we have provided suggestions but there may be other correct answers.

Page 90

1. Any two from: crown jewel; gem; paradise
2. personification
3. The island is loved by the sun; the sun is a welcomed attraction of the island.

Page 91

4. **b** Famous people go there for dinner.
5. It wants to make the island attractive as a holiday destination. *Example answers*: The weather is very good; there is lots to do; tourists can get away from it all.
6. *Example answers*: The weather is guaranteed; there is a wide variety of things to do. There are nice restaurants.
7. *Example answers*: 'just for you' makes the island seem exclusive; 'turquoise waters' make it sound attractive; 'gate to paradise' suggests that this will be more than an ordinary vacation.

Page 92

1. Text types:
   online encyclopaedia = B
   text message = E
   children's story book = C
   school text book = F
   letter from a bank manager = D
   informal email = A
2. Students' own answer.
3. Suggestions for features of a formal letter are:
   - formal register
   - factual content
   - layout that obeys the rules of formal letters (Dear Sir, etc.)
   - business-like tone.
4. Students' own answer.

Page 94

1. **a** He's <u>dissatisfied</u> with his job and wants <u>to leave</u>.
   b She's <u>been miserable</u> since her grandmother got sick.
   c He's got to <u>make a decision</u> on this matter.
   d She's a <u>nuisance</u> who doesn't know what to do.
   e My dad went <u>was angry</u> when the car broke down.
   f He <u>stopped work</u> and went home.
   g She <u>ruined her chances</u> when she failed to turn up to the interview.
   h It's a <u>fuss about nothing</u>.
   i My new computer cost me <u>a lot of money</u>.
   j An opportunity like this comes along <u>infrequently</u>.
2. and
3. Students' own answers.

Page 96

Students' own answers.

Page 97

1. main idea
2. evidence
3. evidence and analysis
4. evidence and analysis
5. evidence and comment
6. transition
7. main idea

Page 98

E, B, D, C, A

Pages 98–99

Students' own answers.

Pages 102–103

1. *fugitive, hunted*
2. *embodiment = personification, incarnation, example of*
3. The use of *significantly* suggests that the gesture was full of meaning or importance.
4. metaphor
5. Describing the characters as standing *like trees* shows that they were still and seemed rooted to the spot.
6. The main points of comparison and contrast are:
- dark and light (creates atmosphere over two paragraphs)
- the natural and the man made, represented by the trees and the road
- both the men being still (creates tension)
- Brower's nervousness; the other man's seeming self-possession (contrast of character)
- stillness and movement.

Pages 104–105

Students' own answers.

Chapter 6

Page 107

1. everyday language and suitable for conversation
2. a verb and a noun
3. *Example answer*: He doesn't handle himself well under pressure.
4. *Example answer*: My new car is not very responsive.
6. *handleless*
7. an adjective
8. He didn't steal the goods himself, but he has been trying to sell them or pass them on to others.
9. It is from Old English and therefore has been in the language for a long time.
10. and
11. Students' own answers.

Page 108

Students' own answers.

Page 109

1. a gate
   b paradise
   c crown jewel
   d sun-kissed
   e creates a list
   f getting the readers involved by asking them to imagine that they are already there
   g the text is easy to approach
   h the different aspects of the island are clearly contrasted.

Pages 110–111

4. a The clarinettist was very healthy.
   b My broken leg is giving me a lot of trouble.
   c We need to think of fresh ideas to solve this problem.
5. a If your eye falls on a bargain, pick up the bargain.
   b If the baby won't eat the food, throw the food away.
   c He gave food to her cat.
   d The girl looked at the boy who had a telescope.

Pages 112–113

1. a annual
   b personally
   c hot
   d in the morning
   e in my opinion (or leave this phrase and cross out *I think*)
   f in succession
2. a Currently, the factory work force is jeopardising our chances of selling our products.
   b The participants were tested in quiet conditions.
   c As it is raining, it is not clear when play will re-start.
3. The organisers of the public display should try to achieve greater safety ~~both~~ **by** ~~from the point of view of~~ ensuring that the bonfire itself does not contain any ~~unacceptably~~ dangerous materials such as ~~discarded~~ aerosol cans or foam furniture and ~~from the point of view of~~ **by** ensuring the letting-off of fireworks in the designated area only. Easily identifiable wardens ~~to be~~ **should be** available ~~during the event~~ to prevent people indiscriminately letting off fireworks~~, to the possible danger of people attending the event~~.
4. (See the amended version in question 3 answer.)

Glossary

Active voice – Verbs are active when the subject of the sentence (the agent) does the action. *Example: The shark swallowed the fish.* Active verbs are used more in informal speech or writing.

Adjective – An adjective describes a noun or adds to its meaning. They are usually found in front of a noun. *Example: Green emeralds and glittering diamonds.*

Adjectival phrase – When two adjectives are used together. *Example: tall and handsome.*

Adverb – An adverb adds further meaning to a verb. Many are formed by adding -ly to an adjective. *Example: slow / slowly.*

Adverbial phrase – A group of words without a verb that functions as an adverb. It tells the reader when, where or how something happens. *Example: I'm going to the dentist **tomorrow morning** (when); The teacher spoke to us **as if he was in a bad mood** (how); Sam ran **all the way home** (where).*

Alliteration – This occurs when two or more nearby words start with the same sound. *Example: A slow, sad, sorrowful song.*

Antecedent – The person or thing to which the pronoun refers back. *Example: President Alkira realised that his life was in danger.* 'President Alkira' is the antecedent here.

Antonym – A word or phrase that means the opposite of another word or phrase in the same language. *Example: shut* is an antonym of *open.*

Audience – The readers of a text and/or the people for whom the author is writing.

Clause – A group of words that contains a subject and a verb.

> A **main clause** makes sense on its own.
>
> A **subordinate clause** depends on the main clause for its meaning.
>
> An **adjectival clause** is a clause that is subordinate to the subject, and is used to describe it.
>
> An **adverbial clause** is a clause that is subordinate to the main verb.

Cliché – An expression, idiom or phrase that has been repeated so often it has lost its significance.

Cliff-hanger – A dramatic and exciting ending to a chapter, leaving the reader in suspense.

Colon – A punctuation mark (:) used to indicate an example, explanation or list is being used by the writer within the sentence.

Comparative adjective – An adjective used to describe a higher degree of intensity, but not the highest possible (see Superlative adjective). *Example: braver; more fiercely*

Compound noun – A noun made up of two or more existing words. *Example: cat food* or *playgroup*

Conditional tense – This tense is used to talk about something that might happen. Conditionals are sometimes called 'if' clauses. *Example: If it gets any colder the river will freeze.*

Conjunction – A word used to link clauses within a sentence such as: *and, but, so, until, when, as.* A subordinating conjunction always belongs at the beginning of a subordinate clause.

Connectives – A word or a phrase that links clauses or sentences. Connectives can be conjunctions. *Example: but, when, because.* Connectives can also be connecting adverbs. *Example: then, therefore, finally.*

Idiom – A colourful expression which has become fixed in the language. It is a phrase which has a meaning that cannot be worked out from the meanings of the words in it. *Example: 'in hot water' means 'in trouble'.*

Intransitive verb – A verb that does not have an object. *Example: The baby was crying.*

Inversion – A reversal of the normal order of words for effect.

Irregular verb – A verb which does not follow the standard grammatical rules. Each has to be learned as it does not follow any pattern. *Example: 'catch' becomes 'caught' in the past tense.*

Metaphor – A figure of speech in which one thing is actually said to be the other. *Example: This man is a lion in battle.*

Modal verb – Verbs that express necessity, possibility, intention, or ability using *must, shall, will, should, would, ought (to), can, could, may,* and *might.*

Parallelism – The use of successive verbal constructions in poetry or prose which correspond in grammatical structure, sound, metre or meaning.

Paragraph – A group of sentences (minimum of two, except in modern fiction) linked by a single idea or subject. Each paragraph should contain a topic sentence. Paragraphs should be planned, linked and organised to lead up to a conclusion in most forms of writing.

Parenthetical phrase – A phrase that has been added into a sentence which is already complete, to provide additional information. It is usually separated from other clauses using a pair of commas or a pair of brackets (parentheses).

Passive voice – Verbs are passive when the subject of the sentence has the action done to it. *Example: The fish was swallowed by the shark.*

Personification – A figure of speech used to give an animal or an abstract item the characteristics of a human. *Example: I was looking Death in the face.*

Prefix – An element placed at the beginning of a word to modify its meaning. Prefixes include: dis-, un-, im-, in-, il-, ir-. *Examples: impossible, inconvenient, irresponsible.*

Preposition – A word that indicates place (on, in), direction (over, beyond) or time (during, on) among others.

Prepositional phrase – A phrase made up of a preposition and a noun phrase, used to give more information about a noun. *Example: The girl in the blue dress was eating an apple.*

Pronoun – A word that can replace a noun, often to avoid repetition.

> **Subject pronouns** act as the subject of the sentence: I, you, he, she, it.
>
> **Object pronouns** act as the object of the sentence: me, you, him, her, it, us, you, them.
>
> **Possessive pronouns** how that something belongs to someone: mine, yours, his, hers, its, ours, yours, theirs.
>
> **Demonstrative pronouns** refer to things: this, that, those, these.

Rhetorical question – This type of question does not require an answer but serves to give the speaker an excuse to explain his/her views. *Example: Who wouldn't want to go on holiday?*

Register – The appropriate style and tone of language chosen for a specific purpose and/or audience. This can be formal or informal.

Relative clause – A type of subordinate clause that describes or explains something that has just been mentioned using the pronouns *who, whose, which, where, whom, that,* or *when. Example: The girl who was standing next to the counter was carrying a small dog.*

Relative pronoun – A pronoun that takes an idea and relates it to a person or a thing (*who, whose, which, where, whom, that,* or *when*). *Example: I talked to your teacher, who told me about your unfinished homework.*

Semi-colon – A punctuation mark (;) that separates two main clauses. It is stronger than a comma but not as strong as a full stop. Each clause could form a sentence by itself. *Example: I like cheese; it is delicious.*

Sentence – A group of words that expresses a complete thought. All sentences begin with a capital letter and end with a full stop, question mark or exclamation mark.

> **Simple sentences** are made up of one clause. *Example: I am hungry.*
>
> **Complex sentence** are made up of one main clause and one, or more, subordinate clauses. A subordinate clause cannot stand on its own and relies on the main clause. *Example: When I joined the drama club, I did not know that it was going to be so much fun.*
>
> **Compound sentences** are made up of two or more main clauses, usually joined by a conjunction. *Example: I am hungry and I am thirsty.*

Simile – A figure of speech in which two things are compared using the linking words 'like' or 'as'. *Example: In battle, he was as brave as a lion.*

Suffix – An element placed at the end of a word to modify its meaning. Suffixes include: -ible, -able, -ful, -less. *Example: useful, useless, meaningful, meaningless.*

Superlative adjective – An adjective used to describe the highest or a very high degree of intensity (Example: *bravest*)

Synonym – A word or phrase that means nearly the same as another word or phrase in the same language. Example: shut is a synonym of close. Synonyms and antonyms can be used to add variation and depth to your writing.

Transitive verb – a verb that is used with an object, *Example: I admire your courage.*

Tricolon (or rule of three) – When a series of three words, phrases or clauses are used together for effect.

Topic sentence – The key sentence of a paragraph that contains the principal idea or subject being discussed.

Index